RAISED BY AN ANGEL

RAISED BY AN ANGEL

DUDLEY E. FLOOD

AuthorHouse™
1663 Liberty Drive
Bloomington, IN 47403
www.authorhouse.com
Phone: 1-800-839-8640

© *2013 Dudley E. Flood. All rights reserved.*

No part of this book may be reproduced, stored in a retrieval system, or transmitted by any means without the written permission of the author.

Published by AuthorHouse 4/3/2013

ISBN: 978-1-4817-1462-4 (sc)
ISBN: 978-1-4817-1461-7 (e)

Library of Congress Control Number: 2013905303

Any people depicted in stock imagery provided by Thinkstock are models, and such images are being used for illustrative purposes only. Certain stock imagery © Thinkstock.

This book is printed on acid-free paper.

Because of the dynamic nature of the Internet, any web addresses or links contained in this book may have changed since publication and may no longer be valid. The views expressed in this work are solely those of the author and do not necessarily reflect the views of the publisher, and the publisher hereby disclaims any responsibility for them.

INTRODUCTION

Raised By An Angel was written as a tribute to my family, my hometown, and especially to my mother. It is my intention to emphasize the fact that a great range of possibilities await our young people if they will but seize the opportunities that are available to them. They must realize that through hard work and persistence, they can achieve whatever goals they may set for themselves.

Each of us must make a personal choice about the advice we receive, the influences to which we respond, and about the priorities that we establish for our life's direction. We may not all become giants in our chosen field or profession, but we can all lead a productive and rewarding life if we will establish a simple and clear direction and commit to following that direction.

I hope that the readers of this book will recognize the joy that simple things can bring to us. In so doing, we will gain renewed appreciation for the blessings that we can be to each other. When we have each other and faith in God, we are rich in every way that matters.

The Flood Family

Having grown up in a small town was once seen to have been a handicap. However, for me it was a blessing. The town of Winton, North Carolina was the ideal setting in which to have been nurtured toward success in life. This was a town that prized its children, and everyone there accepted responsibility for all the children with respect to their upbringing. Added to that fact was the good fortune that I enjoyed to have had five sisters, three brothers and a father, although my father died when I was only fourteen.

The greatest blessing that was to be mine was that of having a mother who was an angel sent from God to do His work in Winton. To have been reared in her love was the greatest gift of all. I know of no person who has ever spoken ill of my mother, and I never heard her speak negatively about anyone else. She found great joy in helping others and was always at peace with whatever situation life presented. She was grateful for little things that most of us see as our reasonable portion of this world's abundance. She loved each of her children, and she treated each in accordance with his or her particular needs.

Each child in our family had the same love and admiration for mother that I had, and each was influenced by her to some degree. In my case, I wanted more than anything in the world to be a son of whom she would be proud. I felt that she had sought so little for herself and had given so much to others that the least she deserved was to have us make her proud. That single motivation shaped my childhood.

Within our family, there were eleven distinct personalities. Out father was a complex personality, capable of showing great love and compassion, but equally capable of confronting anyone who he perceived to have violated his dignity. He was a hard worker, taking great pride in the fact that he provided a reasonable level of subsistence for his family. While we were not affluent, we never thought of ourselves as being poor.

Mother was soft-spoken and easy-going. She never raised her voice through anger, either at her children or at anyone else. She was philosophical in her approach to living. She had hundreds of sayings which helped me to frame my way of thinking. In times of strife, she would say, "This too will pass." In times of trial, she would turn to her belief that God never allows there to be placed upon you more than you can bear. In times of celebration, she would say, "We have done nothing to deserve this." She taught us that the sole purpose of life is to serve and to aid your fellow humans.

Minnie was my most important role model during my childhood years. She was the oldest of the nine Flood children. She began her teaching career the same year that I entered first grade, so I related to her as a teacher as well as an older sister, either of which would have been sufficient reason to follow her example and advice. Minnie took a special interest in my academic and social development. She instilled in me the desire to achieve and the confidence to reach beyond the limited opportunities that were evident in my social environment in that era. The fact that she went to college with no visible support from any source except her own initiative was a vivid demonstration that hard work and focus on a goal were the keys to success. For that insight, I shall forever be indebted to Minnie. At the time of this writing, Minnie has enjoyed ninety-six years of life.

Minnie was married to William David Reynolds of Ahoskie, North Carolina. She is the mother of one son, Roy Gilbert Reynolds of Cary, North Carolina.

Henry, the oldest of the Flood boys was a very special brother. He was large in stature, but had an even larger heart. Weighing thirteen pounds at birth, he was referred to by everyone as the "big boy". Over the years, people dropped the word big and he became known simply as "Boy Flood", a name that would follow him throughout the rest of his life.

"Boy" was my greatest protector. I felt very safe from all physical harm just because he was my big brother. He was recognized as being the strongest man in Winton. I saw him pick up the rear end of an automobile that had gotten stuck in mud. I recall an occasion on which my brother James and I went with "Boy" to see a bear that had been caught by some local hunters.

The bear had been put in a cage and placed on exhibit on the grounds of Felton's Esso station. While we were there, someone opened the cage inadvertently and the bear escaped. The bear was headed directly toward James and me when, to the bear's great surprise, "Boy" Flood tackled it and placed it in such a neck hold that the other men had to rescue the bear from "Boy's" grasp. After that episode, word spread quickly around town that if you see "Boy" Flood fighting a bear, prepare yourself to help to bear. My brother Henry passed away at the age of eighty one in the year 1996. Henry never married.

Virginia Dare was the third Flood child. Being one of only two members of the family to have had more than two syllables in her first name, she had no chance of being called by that name. She was given the benefit of both her initials as she was called "Vee Dee".

"Vee Dee" was the motherly family member. She was the nurturer and supporter of all those with whom she came in contact, whether they were family or stranger, but she was particularly instrumental in my development. It was she who taught me to read and to recite poetry and to love music. The first song that I learned was her favorite hymn that contained the words, "where shall I be when that first trumpet sounds". I haven't heard that song in recent years, but it made a pretty profound impression on me as a three-year old child. Virginia later was married to Floyd Burford of Midlothian, Virginia and to that union was born two daughters, Geneva McCrae and Willa Trinette. Virginia died of cancer in the year 1971.

Ashley was the second male child and the fourth overall in the Flood family. Brother Ashley was an active child, and was always on the move. Like most of the rest of my family, he earned his nickname early in life and it stuck with him thereafter. Ashley, being so active, always wore out his shoes more quickly than our economy could support. On one occasion, he wore out the stitches that held the sole of his shoe. This allowed the sole to flap as he walked. The other children found this funny in that as he walked the flapping sole seemed to be saying "pip-pap, pip-pap". The label, "pip-pap" soon was attached to Ashley, but as time passed, the "pap" was dropped and he became simply "Pip" Flood, the name by which he would be addressed for the rest of his life.

"Pip" had an incredible sense of humor. He was also a practical joker and no family member was exempted from being the target of his pranks. Even when you expected him to play a prank, he still seemed to surpass your level of preparedness for it. For example, once when we were about to enjoy a meal of country vegetables and hog chitterlings, "Pip" sneaked a grain of corn from his pocket and placed it on the side of his plate. He then made the point that the chitterlings may not have been well cleaned. Needless to say, this had a chilling effect on the appetites of my sisters. I found the whole thing disgusting, though I did enjoy the second helping of chitterlings that I got.

Ashley married Ernestine Ford who had four children at the time of their marriage; Ruby Ford, Peggy Ford, Barbara Bowser and Joseph Bowser. To their union, four children were born; Sonya Flood, Virginia Dale Flood, Westly Flood and Andrea Flood. Ashley died of a massive heart attack in 1991 at the age of 69.

Nancy was the next Flood child to arrive. "Pip" was especially fond of Nancy, but they were opposites in personality. "Pip" was an extrovert, while Nancy was an introvert. "Pip" was gregarious while Nancy was retiring. "Pip" was flippant while Nancy was pensive. Still, they were the very best of friends.

Nancy was the quiet family member, so much so that "Pip" gave her the nickname, "Mickey Mouse". We later dropped the "Mouse" and she was just known as "Mickey". In our house there were always two or three conversations going on simultaneously. Nancy would never force her way into a discussion and fight for airtime like the rest of us did. She would wait patiently for her turn to speak. Generally, by the time she would have gotten the floor, "Vee Dee" and "Willie Bea", our other sister, would have gone on to another topic.

Nancy had a beautiful singing voice which she tried hard to hide. She sang only when she thought no one was listening. Even into her adult years, she remained shy and timid, traits that were uncharacteristic for a Flood.

Nancy married Oris Dillard Hall of Ahoskie, North Carolina and to this union two sons were born; Larry Reginald Hall and Oris Rocco Hall. Nancy died of a massive heart attack and of complications resulting from a long battle with cancer in 2009 at the age of 86.

Willie Beatrice, the sixth child was the most dominant personality among the nine. "Bea" was very much a take charge type, offering advice freely and always organizing and planning family activities and telling the other family members what roles they were to play. She had an unlimited supply of energy and a consummate sense of civic responsibility.

"Willie Bea" had been given our father's first name, and she never cared for it, preferring to be called "Bea". I never understood why my pop had passed up the opportunity to give his name to either Henry or Ashley. I certainly would have liked to have been "Bill, Jr.", but I gathered that he had reasoned that "Bea" would have been the last Flood child. I am glad that he was wrong about that assumption.

"Willie Bea" was married to Turner Anderson of Ahoskie. She was the victim of a fatal automobile accident and passed away in 1979.

Josephine, the seventh child was born at the right time in the right place. She was young enough to qualify for nurturing by Minnie and "Vee Dee", and old enough to be "Willie Bea's" best friend. I admired the bond that was evident between "Jo" and "Bea". They were very different in temperament, but each drew strength from the other.

"Jo" was a good student and was active in every aspect of school and community life. She wrote her own life's script and lived life on her own terms. If anything got under her skin, she hid it well. "Jo" was well liked by adults and respected by her peers. I believe that I received a good bit of undeserved attention just because I was "Jo" and "Bea's" little brother.

Josephine married Walter Bernard Whiting of Richmond, Virginia and to this union were born Walter Bernard Whiting, Jr. and Vanessa Louise Whiting. Josephine lives in Richmond, Virginia.

I, the eighth child was given the name Dudley Eargith. Both names were borrowed from persons that my parents knew. I particularly liked Eargith, but it was so frequently mispronounced that even in grammar school, I became "Dudley E". To my surprise, that did not end the mispronouncing of my name. Even today, I am called on occasion

"Douglas", "Dugley", "Dubley" or "Dully". If whatever I am called is close enough to my name for me to recognize that I am being addressed, I answer.

My recollection of my personality is that I was fun-loving, carefree and loquacious. I had a reasonable amount of academic capability and was a gifted athlete. I had a quick wit and was an excellent storyteller. I wanted very badly to be a child of whom my parents would be proud, and to be a good brother to my siblings. I was never sure of whether I met my father's approval, because he never expressed any of his feelings to me, but I was certain that I was my mother's favorite child. I am sure that each of the others felt that they were her favorite. She had a way of making each of us feel very special.

After having graduated from North Carolina College, now North Carolina Central University, I went back to my hometown to begin my teaching career. In my second year out of college, I married my college sweetheart, Barbara Gwendolyn Thomas of Burlington, North Carolina. We had no children, but there are a massive array of nieces and nephews, as well as, all the children that we made a part of our family through the years.

The ninth child, James Edward, was born when I was four years old. I was glad that I would no longer be the baby and that I would have someone to be my best friend. Ashley was nine years older than I, and "Jo" and "Bea" were always doing girl things, so I felt pretty much isolated until James came along. We hit it off right away.

James was an active child, always opening things and pulling down anything that he could reach. I always thought that he was more favored by our father than was I, so it was always he who would ask permission for us to do things. He was fairly well-behaved, but he got into a lot more trouble with mother than I did.

As we grew into our formative years, James and I grew very close to each other. The thing that brought us so close was the condition of our brother "Boy" whom we both loved very much and who needed us throughout his adult life. My brother "Boy" always lived at home. Because of his illness, epilepsy, he was incapable of living independently. Although he managed his own affairs until his declining years, James and I did our best to see that he knew that we respected the contributions that he had made to our early development and that he was still our big brother no matter what may have been his circumstances. Of course, all the family members loved and cared for "Boy", but because James and I had been his roommates as we grew up, we may have known him in a different light than did the other family members. That common experience helped to build a special relationship among the three of us.

James married Hilma Bowser of Portsmouth, Virginia. He and "Peaches" as Hilma is known, resided in Winton until his death in 2006. They had no children.

I have already made reference to our parents, Willie W. Flood and Vancie Vann Flood. Our father, who was called "Bill", had grown up in Franklin, Virginia. My mother was reared in Winton. My parents lived in Southampton County, Virginia in the early years of their marriage, but had settled in Winton by the time I was born. I knew little about my Flood relatives from Virginia, having met only my father's mother, Nancy "Nanny" Flood and his half-brother, Levy Catten. Beyond these family members, I have only second hand knowledge of his side of the family. I knew more of my mother's people because they lived in and around Winton.

Our Summer Pastime

Being the eighth of nine siblings, I have no concept of what it is like to be bored. There was never a time during my childhood when there was not some form of activity to claim our attention. Among my fondest memories are the times we spent exploring in the forests that surrounded Winton.

The distance from our house to C. S. Brown High School was a mile and a quarter if one took the regular route. I sometimes shortened that distance by going through certain back yards and across the campus of Winton Elementary School. However, you could stretch that same trip by taking the Jordan Beach road toward Mr. Bryant Askew's house; passing the old railroad bed; through the pine straw cave that was our private hideaway; taking a drink of fresh water from the spring that ran out of the hill; crossing Barfield Road so as to pass the brick hole; through the Watfords' backyard; and then through Mr. Reynolds' farm and on to school. This was the route that we had created for our own recreational tour. We never took it when school was in session, but during the summers, we spent many happy days in those woods.

We knew every inch of the woods that surrounded Winton, and all our friends knew that if they came to play with us, they would likely play in those woods. We had a favorite spot on the Chowan River bank known as Jordan's Beach. Our house sat about three hundred yards from the river, and we had developed pathways along the river's bank that led to various play sites. One of these sites was the hill that led down to the river onto Jordan's Beach.

On the Jordan's Beach hillside, we cleared the landscape leading down to the river and then covered it with a heavy coat of pine straw. Using fenders taken from old deserted cars that we found at the town dump, we made sleds. We would get into the fender that was turned with its topside toward the ground and this homemade toy would take us for the hundred-yard ride from the top of the hill into the river. The bad news was that the fender would not float, so all of us were forced to learn to swim at an early age.

The wooded areas around our community were so abundant that we as children never concerned ourselves about who owned the land on which we played. We felt both safe and free to play anywhere and to take from the woods whatever raw materials we needed to build our toys and playground equipment. We never took more than was needed nor did we ever damage the environment. Indeed, we frequently cleared the streams that flowed into the river as a part of our playing. We gathered dead twigs to make our fires for cooking and for building our caves and huts. A fallen tree would become our diving board and branches gathered from other dead trees would be used to make a raft on which to explore the river.

The children that played with us came from many different backgrounds and sets of experiences. It was common practice for persons who had grown up in the Winton area and had since moved away to send their own children to live with relatives for the summer. The activities that we created seemed to hold a special fascination for the city boys who came south, especially for those who had never had a rural experience. Donald Reynolds and Collis Turner were the two city boys who spent the most time playing our games with us. Collis was known as "Bookie" Manley because he lived with his grandparents who were Mr. and Mrs. Willie D. Manley, Sr. "Bookie" was a few years older than Donald and he adjusted better to rural living than did any of the other city boys who came down south. I counted him among my closest friends.

Robert Jordan lived on a street paralleled to our street, but which was separated by several acres of wooded land through which ran a large drainage ditch. To reach Robert's house the conventional way, we could walk several blocks of unpaved street, or we could do it the hard way, which was to go through the woods and across the drainage ditch at whatever point we could get across. We nearly always did it the hard way. So did Robert who from time to time would appear as if from out of nowhere.

Robert Jordan was a particularly active boy. He enjoyed wrestling even when no one else wanted to wrestle. It seemed that Robert was always being chased by someone for something that he had done. No one ever actually caught him, because when Robert was being chased, he would run through people's houses to avoid whoever was chasing him. He wouldn't necessarily know the people who lived in a particular house nor would he knock on their door, as was the custom at that time. He would just open their door and run in. Naturally, that would usually end the chase.

People were always moving in and out of our neighborhood on the river hill. Most of our neighbors had no children who were my age. Ulysses Manly, a neighbor who stayed for a good while on the hill, had six children, all of whom were younger than I was. Lois and Lula were old enough to play ball with us, and Lula could swing a pretty mean bat. Lois was a little less likely to join in our games. Donnie, the oldest of the Manley boys would follow us around and would try anything that we did. Dupree and James, the younger Manley boys were seldom allowed to play unless we could find no one else; and Jane, the baby girl was too young to follow us around. Lois and Lula also joined in the football games and the fishing and swimming treks. They were accepted as members of the gang.

Porter "Nub" Spratley and his wife, Mary had one son whose name was Eugene. Eugene never got called by his given name. He was called by some "Lugene" and by others "Nugene". The boys just called him "Gene", which he seemed to like.

"Gene" never seemed to enjoy our company, because he was several years older than the rest of us and he was permitted to smoke. Still, I liked going to his house, because Mary loved children and was an excellent cook. Porter was friendly and outgoing with us children. Besides that, he had a manner of expressing himself that I found entertaining. So "Gene" was stuck with us from time to time.

Selma Burke and his wife, Lillian, were our longest tenured neighbors who had children near our ages. Their oldest child, Logan, who we called "Sonny", was a little more than a year behind me. Gene Elliot or "Bobby" as he was better known was a little behind my brother, James. Then came Fred Allen, known as "Flukie", followed by Lloyd Bennett who we called "Pap", "Squeak", or "Weensy". There was one girl child in the Burke family, but she was not old enough to be a part of our activities. Logan and I did a lot of things together. We bought the same clothes so that we could dress alike. We played the same sports even through our high school years. We hitched rides to Ahoskie and Murfreesboro together, and of course we played in the woods and on the river together.

George and Jake Lee lived directly across the street from us. George was my classmate and was an exceptionally good student. George always played alone. During the hot summer days when the rest of us would be swimming, playing baseball or scouting in the woods, George would set up a mock classroom under the shed in his yard and there he would teach his imaginary students. He always kept a good supply of whips that he had retrieved from the gum tree in his yard. While George required a high standard of conduct from his students, he could at times present quite a challenge to his own teachers at school.

Jake Lee was much more a part of the gang than was George. He was energetic and adventuresome. So, while George taught school, Jake ran with the gang.

The Kearneys lived for a while on the hill. They had one son, Volstead, who we called "Bo Dick". "Bo Dick" was the most interesting of all the neighborhood children in that he was highly animated and spoke in colorful language that he created. For example, he used "diddly-bop" for walk; "nuts and bolts" for car; and "jaw-jacking" for talking. His language would not be seen as out of the ordinary today, but most of us at that time used little if any slang, so "Bo Dick" could hold my attention for long periods of time. He was also given to hyperbole, and even when I knew his stories to have been extensions of his robust imagination, I still enjoyed hearing them.

The Smith family and the Askew family were our most permanent neighbors. Lee Smith was a watch and clock repairman who worked in a shop located behind his house. Mr. Smith was a gentle, soft-spoken man who was always neatly dressed. He and Mrs. Smith had five sons: Joseph, James, Withey, William and Lloyd Allen. They also had two daughters who I remember less well because they never joined in our games.

The Smith boys, though they were not of our race, regularly joined in the activities that we initiated. We were aware that the adults in our community tended to separate themselves along racial lines, but race was much less an issue for us, the children, than was the question of whether one could run, jump, swim or climb a tree. Except for Jim, none of the Smith boys ever raised the issue of race in my presence. Jim did ask us once out of sincere curiosity, "Are you all niggers?" Someone had told Jim that he should not play with "niggers", and he was trying to make certain as to whom they had in mind. I assured Jim that we were not the folks against whom he had been warned.

Alston Askew was my marble-shooting buddy. Alston had a one gallon paint can filled with marbles, and he had a passion for playing marbles. During the winter months, we would draw a ring on the frozen ground in the yard, get down on one knee and execute some very delicate skills in the marble ring. Alston was pretty good at bulls-eye, his game of choice. I was better at the ring version of the game. We also had another version call "holey". In this game, we would dig several holes in the ground, each being two or three inches across (no one measured). The holes would be placed several yards apart, and the object of the game was to shoot your marble into a given hole so that you could advance to the next hole. Then, upon completing all holes, you had to hit your opponent's toy (the term that applied to his marble) to win the game.

Alston's father, Bryant Askew was a gracious and generous man. Mr. Askew owned a farm just up the road from Jordan's Beach on which he raised a very large garden. We always felt welcome to go to his farm and pick vegetables, apples, peaches and pears from his trees and grapes from his vines. He, too, had other children, but Alston was the one that I knew best. Even though I had not seen him for more than fifty years, I still counted him as a friend until he passed away.

Marshall Lee lived in the house at the curve in the road that defined the northern boundary of our neighborhood. His son, Bill, played with our group from time to time, but was not a close friend as were the Smiths and Alston Askew. Bill had a sister who I knew by sight, but with whom I never interacted. It was my opinion that race was a pretty big issue with the Lee children. I may have been wrong about them, but it did not seem worthwhile to pursue that issue. So, we just went our separate ways.

Across the street from Mr. Lee lived Polly Pope and his family. My family felt close to Mr. Pope and his children, and particularly to his daughter, Eva, who was especially outgoing and responsive to everyone around her. My brother, Henry, often worked with Mr. Pope who was a plumber, and they became very dear friends to each other.

On the corner lot that marked the end of our neighborhood stood an elegant, two-story house surrounded by a large, well-manicured yard. In this house lived the only affluent family in our community, except for the Askews who owned a farm. These were the Paramores. Young Tommy Paramore was an extra-special person. He was friendly, outgoing, intelligent, mannerly, and polished. We thought that he was unusually unspoiled for a child of wealthy parents. Tommy seemed not to share the racially divisive attitudes that were so prevalent at that time. He rarely played in the woods with us, but he did come down to the river for an occasional swim. I saw in Tommy great promise of a successful life ahead of him. As it happened, Tommy and I were to remain best of friends until his death. In his adult life, he became one of the best known historians on the history of North Carolina with a major focus on the area in which we grew up. He was a much loved professor at Meredith College and a lecturer for any group who showed an interest in our history.

The Men Who Lived
In the Camps

Our house was the last house on the right of a dead end street that ended at the Chowan River. At the river's edge was a large sawmill that processed the tall pine trees for which our area was known and turned them into lumber. Right next to the sawmill was a lumber chute that was used to move the finished product from the mill onto the cargo ships in the river below.

The slope of the river hill was about fifty yards from the mill to the ships or barges. The lumber chute had a moving cable with sweepers that guided the lumber down to the strong men below who were there to load it manually onto the ships. No machinery was employed in the loading process. Once the ships were loaded, they would travel with their cargo to ports like Norfolk, Virginia and Baltimore, Maryland where their cargo would be unloaded. Then they would be loaded with supplies that they would bring back to Winton.

Beside the lumber chute there was a pulpwood chute. This was a simple boarded incline with sides made of planks that would guide the logs on their downward journey. Pulpwood logs were hauled to the chute directly from the forests from which they had been cut. The cutting, loading and hauling of these logs was a labor-intense operation. Teams of two men using hand pulled crosscut saws did the sawing. In addition, they had to clear away underbrush and defend themselves against snakes, hornets, wasps, mosquitoes and a variety of animals that were not receptive to the encroachment on their natural habitat. A popular saying among the people of Winton was that the prime qualifications for being a pulpwood worker were a strong back and a weak mind.

When the wood reached the river, it would be unloaded from the trucks by hand onto the chute, and it would be taken by hand from the chute and loaded onto the barges in the river. Tugboats would then pull the barges up the river to the paper mill in Franklin, Virginia. Franklin was about thirty miles upstream, but on any day when the wind was blowing from that direction, we could smell the hydrochloric acid and sulfur that was used in the processing of pulpwood into paper. People said that over time you would not notice the smell. I never progressed to that point.

It was the pulpwood and logging industries that spawned the camps on the Chowan River hill. Many of the workers in these industries were recent arrivals to Winton. Most of them had come from Lawrenceville, Virginia or from Franklin where they had previously done a similar type of work. Many had worked for the Chesapeake Camp Manufacturing Company and had found them to be a good employer. Because there was no available housing in our area, the company set up a colony of small one room huts near the river and allowed their laborers to live there rent free. Whether because they belonged to the Camp Company or because of the style of living they provided, I am not certain, we referred to them as "the camps".

Both my father and my brothers, Henry and Ashley, at one time or the other worked in some job that was connected to the logging or pulpwood industry. They knew and worked closely with the men who lived in the camps, and I spent a lot of time around the camps as a result of their relationships. I formed some very special friendships with these men, many of which continued until they either died or moved away from Winton.

The men at the camps lived in such close quarters that their interdependence was a given. They took turns in doing the simple household chores like cooking, washing clothes and cleaning house. They would heat their bath water in a tin tub, which they would place on top of a wood-burning stove. In spite of this inconvenience, it was unusual for one of them to appear in public without having bathed and dressed neatly.

The best cook in the group was Leonard Owens who was known as "Snail". "Snail's" nickname resulted from his deliberate manner of moving and speaking. He used to say," I have two speeds, slow and stop".

"Snail" shared a room with Ceaphus "Bobo" Walker, who was one of my childhood mentors and heroes. "Bobo" eventually would leave the camps and come to live with us. He drove a pulpwood truck and usually did so alone. It was common for two men to staff a truck, because most men could not have lifted the pulp logs onto the truck without help. "Bobo" could do so with ease. He stood just a little less than six feet tall and weighed around two hundred and fifty pounds, all of which appeared to have been muscle. When "Bobo" talked, people listened.

"Bobo" Walker was fond of fishing and of reading comic books, and he taught me to like both these activities. On each payday he would send me to buy comic books for him from Craig's Drug Store. He did not feel welcome in the store that by custom did not serve black people except through a window that separated the main area from the colored waiting room. I gave no thought to going into the store and looking through the comic books to select the books of my choice. It seemed logical to me that one would necessarily scan a book before making the decision to buy it, so I went in less as a revolutionary and more as an enlightened shopper. I heard unflattering comments from time to time, but I was never asked to leave the store.

Several of the men at the camps could not read, so they would have me read aloud to them. I would take such characters as Dick Tracy, Batman, Superman, Captain Marvel, Mutt and Jeff, and the Katzenjammer Kids, and would give them each a voice. If the men found any episode to be particularly funny, they would have me read it over while they enjoyed repeating the words and mimicking the actions of the characters. Making these comic characters come alive constituted my first experience in storytelling. Little did I suspect that storytelling would someday become my profession.

As I think back on the many happy hours that I spent with the men at the camps, I cannot begin to remember all their names, but I do remember how they treated the other children and me. "Bobo" Walker, Les Whitaker, "Snail" Owens, "Big Jack" Alexander, "Red-lipped Shorty", and "Razor-toting Slim" all became members of our extended family. Many of these men would later marry and settle permanently in Winton and would go on to produce families of their own.

In the fall of 1950, I left for college. By that time, the camps were no more. As modern labor methods and technology began to reduce the need for manual labor, a culture disappeared without leaving a trace; a culture that was virtually unknown to people who lived not more than a few blocks from the river hill. Yet, this culture taught me that all people have worth and that all people desire to be treated with respect. Moreover, I came to understand that when you give respect to others, it is more likely that they will give the same to you. These men who lived in sub-standard housing without plumbing, electricity or reliable and adequate heat, and who were employed to use their physical strength, were also proud, gentle and caring people. Their instinct for surviving and for making the best of a less than desirable situation provided a model, which I have found quite helpful throughout my professional career.

School: The Center of Social Life

I began my formal education at the Pleasant Plains Elementary School that sat at a curve in the highway midway between Winton and Ahoskie. This school had two teachers: Ms. Ardell Garrett and Mrs. Viola Chavis. Ms. Garrett taught grades one through four and Mrs. Chavis taught grades five through eight.

The schoolhouse consisted of one building with an outhouse and a hand-operated water pump in its backyard. In its inside, there was a very large room that could be separated into two rooms by the lowering of a portable wall. Sometimes, this wall would be closed to provide some privacy for the respective classes, but as often as not, it was left open while classes were being conducted. This arrangement allowed some of the faster students to get ahead by listening in on the more advanced lessons being taught to their older schoolmates. This was an unplanned benefit, but I certainly profited from it.

I attended Pleasant Plains School for less than a full year. During the early part of winter that year, our family moved into the area served by the Calvin Scott Brown High School, the school from which I would ultimately graduate and at which I was to begin my teaching career.

C. S. Brown High School, as it was later named, had been Waters Normal School and then Waters Training School prior to having been named for its founder, Dr. Calvin Scott Brown. It had been a boarding school for Black students who came from all over the area prior to its having been taken over by the state. The school had a well-deserved reputation for producing an enlightened student population year after year. It was staffed with teachers who lived in the community and who were a part of the lives of their students both in and out of school. They went to church and Sunday School in the neighborhood, sang in the choirs, and directed youth groups such as Boy Scouts, Girl Scouts and 4-H Club. Their influence extended into the total fabric of the community, and they were among the most highly respected of our local civic leaders. In watching these people move about their daily activities, it became clear to me that would be my future profession.

My first teacher at C. S. Brown was Miss Addie Collins. Miss Collins may have been married. Since her marital status was of no interest to me as a child, I have no recollection of what it was. What I do recall is that she was a kind and gentle woman who exercised extreme patience with the children and who seemed to live to teach. She helped to instill in us a love for learning, a love that I carry even until this day.

My second grade teacher was Mrs. Alice Scott who would later become Mrs. Alice Nickens. Mrs. Scott was a very demanding teacher who would accept nothing less than your best effort. She had a way of pushing you beyond the goals that you had set for yourself, but always doing so with such caring that you knew that she had your best interest at heart. Miss Alice, as we addressed her, continued to be an inspiration to me throughout her life. She was my Sunday School teacher for many years, and she was the aunt of Richard Gadsden who would later become my closest friend. These connections combined to create the kind of friendship that is rarely found between today's students and their teachers.

Mrs. Albina Brown Hall taught me in the third grade. "Miss Al" had a daughter, Dawn Brown, who was my classmate and close friend. Because of this fact, I spent more time outside of school with "Miss Al" than with any other of my elementary teachers. We had most of our social gatherings at "Miss Al's" house, and whenever she took her family anywhere, there would likely be several of us tagging along. We ate at her house, studied at her house and went to her for guidance whenever we needed to do so. She was always readily available to help us in any way that she could.

My fourth grade teacher was Mrs. Aline Weaver. Mrs. Weaver was well known as a strict disciplinarian who placed order high within the list of her priorities. She was a stickler for details, and in her room you learned the value of drill and repetition. You learned to memorize all the timetables, to spell everything in the dictionary and that you were never to split a verb. Mrs. Weaver was also our music leader. We had no regular music lessons, but she played for the daily assembly programs and for the many operettas that we presented in elementary school. She also played for the church choir in which I sang and for all the funerals and weddings that were held in Winton. I learned a lot from Mrs. Weaver beyond that which was her job to teach me.

My fifth grade teacher was Miss Sally Bizzell, who later became Mrs. Will Brown. All the students that were fortunate enough to have a class under her guidance loved Miss Sally. She was always able to create a relaxed learning environment in her classroom, and work was more fun than toil. Still, she was demanding and thorough. We began to develop higher order thinking skills in her classroom.

In the sixth grade, Mrs. Lillian Everett was our teacher. She, like "Miss Aline", had developed a reputation for maintaining order at any cost in her classroom. She kept a generous supply of switches handy, but would sometimes add to your misery by having you to go and bring a fresh switch to be used to get and keep your attention. If Mrs. Everett were teaching today, she most assuredly would be arrested for child abuse. However, at that time, we thought that the maintaining of discipline was an integral part of teaching, and that corporal punishment was a logical reinforcer of good behavior. We respected Mrs. Everett, and needless to say, we obeyed her every command. We also learned in her classroom.

My seventh grade teacher was Mrs. Flora Brown Joyner. "Miss Flora", as we called her, was less personable than had been my other teachers up until that time, so I never got very close to her. She was more than adequate at presenting a lesson, and I learned as well in her class as in any of the other teachers' classes, but school became work for me for the first time while I was in the seventh grade. Except for a few high school courses, school would not become work for me again until my sophomore year in college. Still, I am happy that "Miss Flora" was among those who taught me.

In the year that I reached the eighth grade, North Carolina reasoned in its wisdom that eleven grades were insufficient to fully educate the young minds of the day. My class did not go straight from seventh grade into high school as had been the practice in previous years, but instead went to eighth grade in which we became a part of a grand experiment in transitional education.

The concept of eighth grade was not fully developed, but as best as I could understand, it was a cross between high school and grammar school. We had several teachers and we changed classes as did the high school students, but we were treated and were expected to act like elementary children. Of all my schooling, the eighth grade stands out in my mind as having been my least productive and least enjoyable year. In hindsight, I am sure that my own contribution to my development took a one year sabbatical at about that same time, so I fault only myself for that lack of progress.

The High School Years at C. S. Brown

At the time of this writing, sixty-two years have passed since my graduating class left C. S. Brown in May 1950. Still, my memory is more reliable in recalling those years than in bringing back several items from the grocery store on a given day. The impressions that I formed during those years have guided my thinking and behavior in a way that has served me well, and I am most grateful for having had those exposures.

C. S. Brown served not only Winton, but also the surrounding communities, each of which had its own proud identity. The distinctions of the various villages seemed more pronounced when we were children than when we had reached adulthood. Cofield, Tunis, Pleasant Plains, Bluefoot, California and Mount Mariah all sent children to C. S. Brown at the graded school level. Children from Harrellsville, Mapleton,

Murfreesboro and Como joined these at the high school level. Those of us that had begun together in the first grade were to remain together for the full twelve years. Given that fact, we came to know our classmates pretty well over our school careers.

In elementary school, there was a strong element of academic competition among the students. Teachers often gave gold stars to the higher achievers, and each of us wanted to be able to take home several gold stars to show to our parents. We learned to please each teacher through whatever way was necessary in order to earn our gold stars. Some of us did so by working hard. Others did so by kissing up to the teacher. Still others ran a continuing con game on the teachers. We, the students recognized each of these groups for what they were, and we wondered why the teachers seemed not to be able to differentiate.

The small circle in which I competed in elementary school included only boys. Some of the girls did well, but having no relation to them, I did not view them as competitors. I tried to keep up with Ben Watford, Sonny Reid and Junior Jones. All through elementary school, the four of us expected to be ranked first through fourth, with the order varying according to who the teacher was and how she felt about a particular pattern of behavior.

Ben probably was the most capable of us, but he could be expected to lose points for his behavior. He was more inclined than the rest of us to challenge the teacher, and he simply could not resist a dare. I recall on one occasion that I brought a small green snake to school in a glass jar. I dared Ben to put the jar in Mrs. McDougal's desk drawer. It took less than a minute for Mrs. McDougal to conclude that Ben was the culprit, and less than another minute for Ben to implicate me. Needless to say, we both moved down the ladder of esteem which she held for us. We had not been that far up in the first place, and this episode only added to the disenchantment that I had with the eighth grade.

Charles Ray Reid, Jr. was every teacher's dream. "Sonny", as he was called, always did his homework, never missed a day from school, and was well-behaved in class. He was quick to respond when called on, but never spoke out of turn. He was not a wise guy, he dressed well and he carried all his books with him everywhere that he went. We all expected "Sonny" to lead the class in academics, and he rarely disappointed us in that respect.

Arthur Aaron Jones, Jr. was not as studious as "Sonny", but then nobody was expected to be-certainly not "Junior", the fun-loving, free-spirit that he was. I regarded "Junior" as my best friend in elementary school. The first night that I ever spent away from home was spent at "Junior's" house. I sat next to "Junior" in class, and if I knew the answer to a question, I would tell the answer to him since I was too shy to raise my hand. "Junior" responded in class more than anyone else did, because he was speaking for the two of us.

By the time that we reached high school, our circle had begun to expand. We became more aware of the girl students and we began to accept them as rivals for good grades. Among these rivals were Laquitta Hall, Rosa Lee Cooper, Dawn Brown, Aberdeen Watford, Bernice Sawyer, Mary Keene, Valerie Manley and a few others. The whole class was competitive, but these mentioned persons were my closest associates so I recall more clearly those relationships. Ours was a friendly rivalry with each pulling for and being willing to help the others. As soon as our homework papers would be returned to us, we would get together to compare scores and to congratulate those who had done well. The support system that we built was a big factor in our academic success.

Our circle of male students also increased in high school. Sherman Perry came to live with his relatives, Mr. and Mrs. Delaware Jones. Mrs. Jones was our English teacher, and Sherman was a serious student on the same level as was "Sonny" Reid. They became instant friends and as time passed, Sherman became a favorite of most of us. Henry Reynolds, Elton Boone, Roscoe Lassiter, Grady Lassiter, and Pearlie Johnson all joined in the battle for top honors. So did Hollis Porter, Brodie Eley and Clinton Whitaker. Joseph and Henry Britt were good students as well and were generally seen as competitors for the higher grades. To name all the high performing students in our class would require that I virtually call the class role. We had very few non-productive classmates, and all who came to school regularly, did well.

After having survived the eighth grade experience, I found high school to be refreshing. We had six classes each day. So, it was more exciting to be exposed to a variety of teachers than to spend all day in one place with one teacher as was the case in elementary school. It had already become clear to me while in the eighth grade that a major determinate of how well I did in school was the relationship that I managed to form between the teachers and me. I further realized that being the class clown did not contribute positively to the building of viable relationships with the teachers, or for that matter, of being taken seriously by the other students, so I reluctantly resolved to have less fun and to put forth more effort toward being a conventional student. As I began to initiate this change, school took a turn for the better for me. I still enjoyed school, but my enjoyment now became a product of my academic success and social growth, rather than being my primary focus in life.

Most of my high school teachers were excellent teachers. However, there were several that went so far beyond their prescribed area of responsibility to help us students that these persons played a major role in my development. First among these was my first male teacher, Mr. Dennis McCaskill. Mr. McCaskill had taught at C. S. Brown earlier in his career before having left for a tour of duty in military service. He returned from service the same year that I entered ninth grade. I had heard from my older sisters that he was an excellent teacher, but that was only half the story. The more important thing that he was to me was an example of what it meant to be a mentor and role model for someone who was looking for neither.

Having as I did a supportive family and two parents, the last thing I wanted was someone else to mind my business. However, in March of my ninth grade year, my father died of pneumonia. Even though this was a traumatic experience for me, I still had more than a reasonable amount of support from other family members, and had advice coming out of my ears about how to conduct myself and how to grow up properly. Mr. McCaskill did little preaching, but more modeling of the virtues that he sought to instill in his pupils.

"Mr. Mac", as I came to call him, reached an independent conclusion that money was in no great abundance in our household, but he knew as well that we were above accepting much in the way of charity, so he began creating opportunities for me to earn money for myself. He would have me come to his house and shine his shoes, for which he paid me ten cents a pair. I got so good at shining shoes that I soon started my own shoe shine business, a business that kept me in spending money all through high school, and one which stayed in the back of my mind well into adulthood as an alternative to working in an abusive situation. Even now, I enjoy shining shoes.

"Mr. Mac" taught me the value of diplomacy. He relied on his ability to motivate more than on his power to command. Wit and wisdom were combined in his presentations in such a way that one reinforced the other, and I became aware that these were not conflicting concepts. It was comforting to learn that it was appropriate to teach and to have fun at the same time. It was in "Mr. Mac's" classroom that I selected teaching as my chosen profession.

"Mr. Mac" introduced me to organized sports. As a child, I had played baseball every day during the warm months of the year, but our games had been without adult supervision. We played under our own rules and developed our own habits and skills. Sometimes, our rules bore little resemblance to the actual established rules of a particular game, and since we played without officials, the biggest boy who was in the game enforced the rules. "Mr. Mac" was the high school basketball coach during my ninth grade year, and he urged me to come out for that sport.

Prior to my ninth grade year, I had never touched a basketball. My community was the baseball capital of the region. It was the home of three very successful "sand lot" teams as they were called, and the most successful of these three, the Chowan Bees, played its home games in Winton. This team had successfully competed against teams in the Negro League, and its players were our childhood heroes, so football and basketball had taken a back seat to baseball for me. "Mr. Mac" changed all of that. He was my coach for only one year, but during that year, I began a journey that would lead to my becoming one of a handful of pretty good basketball players to come through C. S. Brown during my time there.

Another favorite teacher in high school was Mr. Samuel Lewis. Mr. Lewis taught Plane Geometry, which became my second most favorite subject, second only to English. Mr. Lewis had been disabled to the degree that he taught from a wheelchair, a fact that placed him in a unique category. At that time, disabled people were seldom seen carrying out demanding responsibilities such as teaching school. Mr. Lewis did not allow his disability to diminish his effectiveness as a teacher. He was jovial in and out of the classroom, and he knew his subject matter so well that he rarely referred to notes or opened a textbook. He required that we commit to memory all the theorems and postulates, and that we were able to trace our route to conclusions rather than simply knowing the right answers. He maintained an invitational atmosphere in his classroom in which all but the most disengaged students were able to master a subject that was generally thought to be quite difficult.

Miss Brett was our Biology teacher, and all of us were in love with her. We were disappointed that she soon married and moved away, but she was a special person to us during her time with us. She became Mrs. Oliphant during the year that we were in her class. We had never had a teacher to get married while teaching us, so this was quite an adjustment for some of us. Later, Miss Daniels was to become Mrs. Faison, also to our disapproval, but we were a little better prepared for the idea of our teachers having a personal life by then.

Mrs. Varner taught us French, a subject that was critical to our being accepted into college at that time. It was the only foreign language offered at our school, and Mrs. Varner was the only French teacher, so she had a lot of power over our future and we knew that. Her classroom was the quietest of all those that we attended, and everyone recited, however poorly, and all turned their work in on time. While not learning to speak any of the language, I found some value in having studied French as it did enhance my understanding of language in general. What is more, my self-image was improved in that I felt more intellectual because of that exposure.

Mr. Varner was my Chemistry teacher, and was the football and basketball coach. He had played football at Johnson C. Smith University and had some knowledge of that game, but he was only casually familiar with the game of basketball. Most of what we learned about that sport, we learned on our own. Still, we had one of the better basketball teams in the area.

Mr. Varner was a hard-nosed sort who insisted on being in charge. He was not the least reluctant to go one-on-one with any of the boys who defied his authority. During my junior year, Mr. Varner averaged one scuffle a month with one student or another. Oliver Mike Bynum could be counted on to "get Mr. Varner's goat" about that often, and he would always refuse to leave the room when asked to do so. So, Mr. Varner would always proceed to remove him physically. Sometimes Mr. Varner won, and occasionally we thought the particular student had won. Every now and then, Mr. Freeland, our principal, would have to come over to intervene, but generally the prevailing attitude was that Mr. Varner was just being himself.

Mr. Jarmond was one of my favorite teachers. He taught what was then called Agriculture, but it was much more inclusive than the name would suggest. In Mr. Jarmond's class, we learned about farming and about conservation of our natural resources. We also learned carpentry, brick masonry and painting. We learned horticulture, livestock raising and cabinetmaking.

Mr. Jarmond was the advisor of a subject-related club to which all students of Agriculture belonged that was named New Farmers of America. In "NFA" as it was commonly called, we learned public speaking, debate, and an intricate knowledge of Parliamentary Procedure. All these skills have been particularly useful to me throughout my professional career. Moreover, the skills and knowledge that I gained from studying under Mr. Jarmond enabled me, along with my wife, to build our first house. We purchased a "shell" home which consisted of a framed, closed-in, roofed structure and a package of materials that would be needed to complete the inside of the house. Except for the wiring and plumbing, we did the rest of the work, relying only on the knowledge that I had acquired in high school. It later became the home of a very happy couple who bought it from us when we moved away from Winton. That house was built in 1957, and more than fifty-five years later, it is still standing.

We had other teachers along the way, some of whom I remember just vaguely. Mr. Milton Reynolds taught us Math, Mrs. Coleson taught History and General Science and Miss Copeland taught Math and also played a mean game of horseshoes. Mrs. Brummel, who taught Social Studies, was kind enough to allow me to fulfill my student-teaching requirement under her. So, her teaching had a profound influence on my career. Even our principal, Mr. Freeland, taught a class. His subject was Geography, and though he was frequently called away from class to attend to administrative matters, he was an excellent teacher in whose room I learned a lot. The one teacher that I do remember above all the rest was my English teacher, Mrs. Undean Jones.

Mrs. Jones was the first teacher in whose room I did my best to excel. Before I had her for a teacher, I thought that certain other students were supposed to be at the top of the class, and I performed at the level at which I perceived that I was expected to perform. Mrs. Jones convinced me that I had a special talent in the ability to do well with language, and that she was willing to accept my best work on face value and not in relation to how other students were performing. In her class, I learned the English language so well that in college, I wrote term papers and themes almost without effort. Due to Mrs. Jones' influence, I developed a love for oral expression that helped to lead to my present profession as a public speaker.

Mrs. Jones' nurturing and guidance did not end with her official duties as our teacher. She was always willing to serve as advisor, chaperone and even host for the many out-of-school activities that we initiated. Her nephew, Sherman Perry, who lived with her, was a close friend with whom I spent the night from time to time. Mrs. Jones would always do something special for us after we had done our homework, which was a daily requirement from our teachers. If I had to name the one teacher who made the most positive impact on my life, that person would be Mrs. Undean Jones.

Extracurricular Activities at C. S. Brown

Because our school was literally the center of all our activities, there was always something other than class work taking place at the school. Three of the major annual occurrences were the Popularity Contest, the May Day Program and the Annual Commencement Day Celebration. Each of these activities involved the total community, and along with the fourth major occurrence, Founder's Day, involved every student in the school as well as every faculty member.

In those years, schools for minority children were woefully underfunded, and all schools for Black children regularly held fundraisers to supplement the public monies that flowed from the state and county. The Popularity Contest was C. S. Brown's major fundraiser. Each student at whatever grade level was encouraged to engage in fundraising activities under the leadership of their parents. At the end of the period set aside for the annual drive, all funds would be reported to the principal, and the person having raised the greatest amount would be declared Popularity Contest Queen. The Contest evolved over the years into a competition among classes rather than among individuals. Each class would select its candidate for queen, and the contestant from the winning class would be crowned. Boys were not eligible for that particular honor, but we took great pride in having the winner to come from our class.

The May Day Program was a culmination activity for the drama and production department of the school. While we were not formerly departmentalized as such, the school functioned as if it were. Mrs. Jones, Mrs. Varner, and later Mrs. Brummel were regularly in charge of our dramatic productions. Sometimes Mrs. Faison would help with the production of a high school play. These same people generally had a hand in the production of the May Court, although other teachers helped as well.

The elementary students had a significant role in the May Court. There would always be a May

Pole winding for each of the several grade levels. Since the activity was scheduled to take place on the first of May or the nearest school day thereto, everyone involved dressed in white from head to foot. The activity lasted all day, so the parents who came to the event either brought their lunch from home or they purchased their lunch from one of the many venders that would be set up on the campus for that day. After the formal program had ended, the rest of the day was spent in fellowship, eating and playing on the schoolyard. The yard would always be filled with adults from all parts of the county from which students came. May Day was truly a highlight of our year.

Commencement Day was another grand occasion for the C. S. Brown School community. Generally held on the day immediately preceding graduation, this was also a time when all kinds of people came to spend the entire day at school. This day was even grander than May Day. There would be more vendors and more visitors to the campus on this day. Many out-of-town people came, and the atmosphere was similar to that of the county fair. Whole families would come. People who had moved away from the community would return to town for this gala occasion.

Needless to add, the school made some badly needed money on those days.

An important part of the extra-curricular offerings at C. S. Brown were the dramatic productions. Beginning with the operettas that were put on by the primary grade children through the three-act dramas produced by the high school drama club, there was always an opportunity available for students to appear on stage before an audience. I was in some sort of production every year that I spent at C. S. Brown.

In the lower grades, everyone was in a play regardless of their level of talent, but to make the high school productions was an honor. The faculty advisors selected people who they were sure would learn their lines, show up for rehearsal and keep up their school work while doing so. Acting talent was not so highly regarded as a prerequisite since the advisors were going to insist that the students follow their directions to the letter. Creativity was frowned on, a fact that led to my never having won a leading role in any of the plays.

I was always cast as the character that made the audience laugh. This was generally a very small part of the play, but I had to show up for practice just like everyone else. Sometimes I would sit for hours waiting my time to speak my few lines. Then, I would be finished until the finale when everyone would be brought back on stage, so I had to stay through the whole practice each day. By the time the play would be ready for production, I would know the lines of every character in the play.

Twelve years of playing supportive roles, many times doing so behind people who had less ability than I had, helped to equip me for the roles that I would play in later life. I learned the importance of finding one's own niche and of developing that niche to make it work to your advantage. I learned that the character that plays the minor role is just as essential to the finished product as is the person who gets the greatest applause at the curtain call.

Athletics were not stressed to any great extent during my high school years at C. S. Brown. Although the town in which the school sat was literally a haven for baseball, the school did not have a baseball team. Football had been played there in years past, but it had been discontinued during the period of World War II and was not resumed until my eleventh grade year. Needless to say, we were severely disadvantaged in our ability to compete against schools who had a more recent legacy of football exploits. We had no role models, no heroes, nor very much in the way of coaching. In short, we were not a very good team.

My football career lasted for only my junior year. At the beginning of my senior year, I was advised by Dr. Joseph D. Weaver that a heart murmur that I had carried since age fourteen had worsened to the point that I should not participate in football. This came as no great disappointment to the coaches, given the level of contribution that I had made. However, I did remain with the team as a non-playing member, a role in which I learned more about the game than I might have learned had I been concentrating on one position.

Basketball was the only other sport offered at C. S. Brown. We had no gymnasium, so our home games were played outside. Since our practices were also held outside, we had a great advantage when playing at home. In fact, we never lost a home game during my playing years. However, some teams declined to play on our outdoor court and we played both games in their gym. Our archrival, R.L. Vann of Ahoskie, enjoyed the home court advantage for each of the years that I played. We never won a game over Vann during those four years.

Prior to my ninth grade year, I had not found basketball attractive. Baseball was my sport of choice until Mr. McCaskill introduced basketball to me. C. S. Brown had dropped basketball for a few years, but as the boys who had served in the military during the war began returning to school to complete their formal education, the sport was resumed.

During my freshman year, most of the starting team consisted of veterans of the military. The starters were Sidney Britt, Clifton "Sonny" Eley, Randolph Strayhorne, James Wilkes and Jesse Simmons. Jesse was the only regular who had not been in the armed services. All these players were seniors, so the rest of us had a full year to practice against them and to learn from them. Sidney Britt, the best athlete in our school, had a romantic interest in my sister, Josephine, and he spent a good bit of time teaching me what he knew about sports. I substituted for Sidney whenever he would come out of a game, which was not often, but when I would get to play for a few minutes, Sidney would watch me and would later advise me on how to improve. When he graduated, I became a starter and continued to start every game that we played for the next three years.

During my sophomore year, we had only one senior on the team, Jesse Simmons, who played center. The younger players were becoming more comfortable with their leadership roles. Henry Reynolds and I were named co-captains of the team, and we continued in those positions through the following three years. Buck Harrell was the starting point guard. Buck was noted for his quickness and for his exceptional foot speed. Clinton Boone became the starting center. "Clint's" strength was his ability to make the outlet pass. He would take a defensive rebound off the backboard and with one motion release a line-drive pass to a player who was all the way under the basket at the other end of the court. Elton Boone played the wing position. He was a pretty good ball handler and could make a lay-up shot. Henry Reynolds and I did most of the scoring from our forward positions.

Mr. Varner was head basketball coach. He had a very fixed approach to the game, which consisted of moving the ball around until you could get an easy shot from inside the free throw line. The problem that approach presented was that we had a very small team. "Clint" Boone, our center, was barely six feet tall. Our back-up center, Hunter Lane, was the only other six-foot player on the team after Jesse Simmons graduated. Purcell Bowser was our best player off the bench, but he was five feet, nine inches. Buck Harrell was about the same, and Henry was about five feet, eleven inches. I was the next tallest at five feet, ten and a half inches. The other players on that team included Lloyd "Tiny" Jones, Adron Jones, Jr., "Sonny" Reid, Logan Burke and Clarence Scott.

In watching from the sidelines all during my freshman year, I concluded that due to my lack of bulk and height, I would not be getting many inside shots, so I developed an outside jump-shot as well as a set-shot. I worked hard at developing those shots and I became quite good at them. Mr. Varner had no confidence in that part of my game, believing that luck was the determining factor in whether I would make such a shot. From time to time, I would put one up from the half court line hitting nothing but net, hoping to convince him that some skill was involved in shooting from outside the lane. Though I made more of those shots than I missed, he never changed his mind about my shot.

In the years to come, many players at Brown were to become good shooters. The very year following my graduation, Purcell Bowser led the conference in scoring with his outside shot being his primary tool. Adron Jones and Osborne Porter became good shooters after my playing years. I think that Mr. Varner may have taken a second look at the jump shot during their playing years. I wondered if he had ever reflected on the fact that I had started that tradition with no encouragement from him.

The Scholastic Competition at Elizabeth City State

A highlight in our school year was the scholastic competition that was held each year at Elizabeth City Teachers College. Students who were leaders of their classes in subject areas would engage in competition with students from other schools from around the area. The students would be given standardized achievement tests particular to the respective subject in which they would be competing, and prizes would be awarded for the highest score and for the second and third place finishers in each category. Any student who was selected by his or her teacher to participate in the competition could expect to receive some focused attention from that teacher prior to going to Elizabeth City, because the honor of C. S. Brown was at stake during that competition.

I was privileged to have been selected for the contest in each of my four years. This was somewhat surprising in that mine was not among the three highest grade point averages in my class. Still, in my four years of competing, I won three first places and one second place in the overall competition. I always felt that my strongest competition would come from my other team members from C. S. Brown, and this proved to be true in that we frequently brought back honors in all three places. The competition in academics was discontinued shortly after my class had graduated, and many of us believed that it was dropped because other schools no longer were willing to take that annual whipping from C.S. Brown.

Building Friendships During My High School Years

I have always valued friendship quite highly, and I have been fortunate to have had some loyal and devoted friends over the years. Like most other people, I have also been involved in some one-sided friendships with people who took and never gave. I would like to think that I learned from the latter, but even today I do not pick my friends based on what they may do for me. If I did so, I would be even more of a loner than I am.

Upon reaching high school, I discovered that friends from elementary school developed new interests and drifted apart. "Junior" Jones, who had been my best friend in graded school, began to have other friends to whom he was closer. My playmates from the river hill had all moved away or formed other bonds, so I was faced with the challenge of forming new friendships for the first time in life.

My first set of friends developed from my participation in sports. Henry Reynolds and Elton Boone were my teammates and my classmates, so we gravitated naturally toward the forming of a strong friendship. Other friendships were less natural. Off the campus, I played baseball with Sherman "Juke" Jones, shot pool with Larry "Bones" Lassiter, hitched rides to wherever with Jimmy Lassiter, and spent the summer days with Collis Turner. Bob Jordan's family moved away, and "Sonny" Burke was the only neighborhood friend that remained. Most of these friendships have persisted at some level through the years, but the most unusual of all and the longest lasting of all my early friendships was that with Richard Gadsden.

Richard was not in our elementary class, so I did not know him very well until my tenth grade year. Richard was friendly with my sister, Josephine, as they were nearer in age and in grade level, two factors that had great relevancy in those days. In my sophomore year, Richard became ill and was confined to his home for more than a year. I visited him a few times along with other peers, and later when some of the others were busy with their own affairs, I still found the time to visit Richard daily. In those months of his confinement, we developed a friendship that was to grow into a virtual partnership over the rest of our formative years.

When Richard recovered from his illness, he returned to school as our classmate. He and I spent our weekends visiting the girls in the area, going to the nightspots, going to church and playing croquette in his yard. We spent our summers waiting tables in Atlantic City, New Jersey, and we even selected the same college to attend. We knew each other so well that if one of us started a story, the other could finish it. Our friendship remained strong through our lives until Richard's passing.

Ben Watford was another special friend. He and I always sat near each other in class so that we could exchange observations on everything that went on in the classroom. Ben was a superior student and an independent thinker. He had a sense of humor that was not always welcomed by our teachers, but he was such a personable young man that teachers tolerated more of his antics than was the custom. Ben and I frequently engaged in mind games such as trying to stump each other with word definitions. Ben liked oration and was very good at it. He also enjoyed poetry, and we would compete with each other to see who could memorize the longest poems in the shortest period of time. In our adult life, Ben taught me to play chess. This seemed right in character for Ben Watford who by then had become a teacher and world traveler.

Many of the girls in our class were friendly, but I never felt particularly close to any of them. I never had a girlfriend that I thought had an exclusive relationship with me. All the girls that I liked seemed to like more mature fellows, so I became everyone's brother. This early experience inclined me to be skeptical of forming intimate relationships with girls, the result of which was that I had my first serious romance when I was a junior in college. As I look back on that situation, that was probably early enough.

Even though I had no exclusive girlfriend like the rest of my peers, there were always girls involved in our social activities, and I enjoyed interacting with them. Mrs. Hall and Mrs. Jones would sometimes host social gatherings, usually at Mrs. Hall's house. The girls most likely to attend these affairs were Mrs. Hall's daughter, Dawn Brown, Bernice Sawyer, Shirley Freeland and Rosa Lee Cooper, each of whom had steady boyfriends most of the time. The boys most likely to be there were Richard Gadsden, Sherman Perry, "Sonny" Reid, "Junior" Jones and me. Other boys were invited on occasion, but we were the regulars. Now and then, Laquitta Hall would attend. These house parties were an unlikely setting for the development of a seething romance. Most of us felt that we were members of the same family in that setting. "Junior" and Laquitta managed to develop a serious affair, but it took about eight years to culminate in marriage. The rest of us remained just friends.

Hertford County's Recreational Offerings

Most of the recreational experiences that bore parental approval were associated with either the school or the church. We had other fun places that we frequented that were not on the approved list. On a typical Friday night during the school year, we would all meet at Sherman Perry's house to study, eat and socialize. On Saturday night, we would get together at Dawn's house where we would listen to records by the hottest groups such as the Orioles, the Platters, the Drifters, the Ravens and the Charles Brown Trio. My favorite artists, Billy Eckstine and Nat "King" Cole, were less popular with the group, but were generally tolerated. Sherman and I liked Sara Vaughan, so her records were allowed. In return, we tolerated artists that some others liked.

On Sunday, after Sunday School and church, we all went to our own homes for the compulsory Sunday dinner with our respective families. As soon as dinner was over, I would head for Richard's house, and the tour of non-approved sites would begin. Our first stop would be Chowan Beach.

Chowan Beach was a major attraction for people from all over eastern North Carolina and southeastern Virginia. It was the only public swimming facility available to Blacks between Sea View Beach on the Chesapeake Bay and North Myrtle Beach in South Carolina. The daytime offerings were oriented to the family. There were rides and vendors, and there was playground equipment for the children. Usually, there would be a lifeguard on duty to care for the safety of the swimmers. However, after sunset, Chowan Beach featured more adult entertainment. Many of the popular performing groups of that era appeared there. Richard and I were too old for the children's activities and too young for the adult entertainment, so we adapted to both and made the best of our situation.

During the winter months when the beach was closed, our favorite haunt was the Casa Mayama. This, too, was an adult entertainment setting, but anyone who could drive a car went there. The "Cass" featured live bands and acts. It had a fairly large dance floor, and on nights when no live show was being featured, the jukebox provided the most popular current selections. In addition to dancing and meeting new people, you could expect to see at least one fistfight on any given Saturday night. Generally, the same folks would do the fighting every time, and seldom did it amount to more than a few blows and a lot of woofing. Still, we had some good talking material when describing it to the girls who were not allowed to go to the "Cass".

Another off-limits spot that we liked to visit was Sam Pilmon's East End Café in Ahoskie. Sam's was smaller than the "Cass", but was just as lively. It tended to draw the pedestrian traffic from the surrounding area. More of the younger group who were under driving age could come to Sam's to act out adult behavior.

If you were from Winton, you were not welcomed by the boys from Ahoskie to become friendly with the girls there, a fact that seemed to prompt the girls to be more than a little assertive toward Winton boys. Richard and I had formed friendships with many of the boys in Ahoskie, and we received a little better than average welcome, but we knew and respected the limit on our interaction with the girls.

Over on the Gates County side was the Triangle, a nightspot also known as "Jordan's Place". Some Sunday afternoons, Richard and I would go to Boone Town to visit a family that included several fairly attractive girls. Honoring the tradition of ending all visitations by ten o'clock on Sunday night, we would leave Boone Town and stop by the Triangle. Nothing much ever happened there, but it added to the litany of exciting tales for us to share with our peer group.

In Winton proper, there were several gathering places that we occasionally dropped in for a brief "look-see", but we knew that these were truly off-limits and that the news of our having been there would reach home before we did, so we avoided these places as a rule. Among these was Clyde Watford's place, which the locals called the Mink Slide Inn, so named by my brother "Pip" Flood. There was "The Hole" and "The Neck" and several private homes that became speakeasies on the weekends. Since no one in our group drank alcoholic beverages, we found these places less appealing than the public places where we could dance, fellowship and spend almost no money in so doing.

Winton Had Its Share of Characters

For a town of its size, Winton was the home of an array of interesting people. Most everyone in the town knew most everyone else, and they were proud of being just regular folks, so no one put up much of a facade. One of my favorite pastimes was to sit and listen to the interaction among adults who were expressing themselves in the uninhibited way that characterized Winton people. One of the gathering places for these conversations was the service station that was owned by Mr. J. Eli Reid.

Mr. Reid was himself an interesting person. He was a generous man who placed a high value on the work ethic. If you were willing to work along with him, he would give you some kind of a job. I spent many hours working for Mr. Reid at his beach property. He also owned a sand hole near his Chowan Beach site, and we often hauled sand from the sand hole to replace that which the tides had washed away from the waterfront. The river was not naturally sandy, so this was an on-going process necessary to maintain the appeal of the swimming area.

Mr. Reid was such an active person that when working with him, there was hardly any work for you to do; he did most of it himself while showing you how it should be done. His pace was full speed all the time, and he never seemed to tire. I greatly admired his approach to getting things done, and I began to appreciate the correlation that exists between hard work and success while working for him.

Mr. H. C. Freeland, our school principal, was someone that I admired greatly and tried to emulate. He showed an unusual interest in the development of his students outside the school setting. He taught in our Sunday School as well as in the Pleasant Plains Church's Sunday School. He gave me a job cleaning the toilets at C. S. Brown after school and paid me at wages equivalent to those that an adult would have earned for having done the same work. Whenever I was in his presence, I felt that I was learning something useful to better my situation. When I grew up, I tried to exhibit that trait to the youth around me.

Miss Aurie Keene, one of my early Sunday School teachers, showed the children a lot of caring. I worked around her house performing chores such as painting, cutting grass, cleaning house and running errands. She always paid well for whatever I did, but on top of that, she would give me money to put in church each Sunday, even if I had not worked for her that Saturday. Our class always won the banner for having had the best collection. We enjoyed the honor, but most of the money came from Miss Aurie Keene.

Mr. Rochelle Vann left Winton when I was a small child and served with honor in the armed services. After the war, he returned to his hometown as a hero. During those days, there were no parades or dinners held to commemorate the deeds of a local hero. You knew what he or she had achieved because the word was spread from person to person. When such a person came back and settled down in the community, there was great joy among our people.

I looked to Mr. Vann as a role model. He took great interest in the development of the boys in Winton. He organized a Boy Scout troop and a Cub Pack and served as Scoutmaster for both. He started a youth club that provided structured activities that were both wholesome and developmental for the children. Further, he set an example through his behavior that I found impressive. In later life, he and I would become close personal friends, and he would eventually inspire me to teach the adult Sunday School class at my home church. For that friendship, I am grateful.

The man that I most respected in our community was Mr. Theodore Hunter. Mr. Hunter lived alone in the servant quarters provided by Mr. John Shaw for whose family he was a domestic servant. He was a deacon of First Baptist Church in Winton, and unless he was ill, which he frequently was, he never missed a church service of any kind. He was loving and kind to all who came in contact with him, and he used every opportunity to teach moral behavior. His mere presence directed my thinking toward doing the right thing. On occasions, I would visit Mr. Hunter at his living quarters. There was a sense of order in his little house. It was filled with things that people had given him over the years, but it was not cluttered. A sense of perfect peace abided in Mr. Hunter's house as in his presence.

Preaching was a highly visible and highly respected field of endeavor during the days of my youth. Winton had only one pastoring preacher that lived in the town and that was the Reverend H. T. Mitchell. There were several other persons who spent time in the pulpit spreading their own brand of gospel, such as Rev. William Henry Vaughan and Rev. Garfield Harcum. Aside from these men, preachers were in short supply from within, so we were always importing someone to fill the local churches' pulpits. Rev. Mitchell preached at our church for a while, but he had other churches and soon they required his full attention.

Over the next several years, we experienced a series of short tenured pastors, so I was never influenced by anyone in the ministry. In fact, I failed to develop the respect that I would have liked to have had for that position. I still until this day lack the ability to unquestioningly follow a person purely because he or she is in the ministry. I have since known some excellent ministers and have come to respect many of them, but my early years did not equip me to serve in that role myself.

Dr. Joseph D. Weaver had a profound influence on the development of the youth during my childhood. Aside from being a successful medical practitioner, he was active and visible in every aspect of community life. He worked hard and he appeared to have enjoyed his work, but when not at work he seemed to enjoy the fruits of his labor more than did anyone else that I knew. He had a place at the beach, his own airplane, a convertible automobile and an array of friends who were willing to contribute to his enjoyment. As my family doctor, he was a frequent visitor in my home, and all my family loved him. I was proud that I was among those that he called friend after our doctor-patient relationship had ended.

In addition to these named people with whom I had a direct relationship, there were others that I admired from a distance. Among these were Miss Marion Reid who taught at C. S. Brown for a short while; Miss Pride, who was just a few years older than her students; Mr. Anderson Pugh from Jordan's Grove Church and Mr. Spurgeon Vann from First Baptist Church. Mr. Eddie Bowens, who sold fresh fish from the back of his pickup truck, was always good for an extended lecture on some issue of the day. The other two Bowens brothers, John and Saint were generally good for a couple of stories about how things used to be. Mr. Buddy Smith, a carpenter, was one of the more clever persons that I have known. He told funny stories and he told stories funny. Mr. Clayton Felton was a stammerer, and though his humor was captivating on its own, he used his stammer to be even more humorous. The list of impressive characters could go on and on, but the few that I have named come to mind more readily because with them, I had frequent contact and was left with good feelings about them.

College Days at Dear Old North Carolina College

During my early high school years, the thought of going to college never occurred to me. In the first place, I never thought farther ahead than a few weeks at best. Secondly, as far back as I could trace my family, only one male child had gone to college. John Wells, my first cousin, had earned a degree, but all the other males had acquired less formal education than that. The family member of whose success I was most aware was cousin Paul Wells, who worked on a train in New York City. I had no concept of what Paul did on the train, but he always seemed to have a lot of money and he seemed happier than anyone else who came down from the city to visit us. I hoped that I might get a job like Paul's so that I could come home when on vacation and bring presents to my family.

At the beginning of my senior year, my sister Minnie sat me down and explained to me that I would be going to college the next year and I should begin to plan accordingly. I could not fathom the possibility of doing so, but I had never known Minnie to engage in idle speculation, so I conceded that she knew of some financial resources unknown to me. It turns out that the money for my education came out of her pocket, and until this day, I do not understand how she managed to do what she did. My sisters Willie Bea and Josephine were both in college at Hampton Institute, a private college that had a higher tuition than did most public colleges. As best I knew, their sole source of help beyond whatever they were able to generate on their own initiative was Minnie. Nancy had completed her college work and had become employed as a teacher, so I am sure that she was helping Jo and Bea, but any way I looked at it, we were walking on very thin ice.

"Bea" and "Jo" had both worked during the summers to earn some money for school expenses. I, too, had had a summer job away from home since the age of fifteen, but the kind of money that I had made would not have gone far toward a college education. However, after it became clear that ending my formal education was not an option, I became more conservative with my earnings, and as a result, I was able to buy all my clothes and personal need items with money that I earned. Minnie provided the money for tuition, room and board, for which I am eternally grateful. I would still like to know her secret for managing money.

The decision as to where to attend college was a simple one for me. I knew by then that I wanted to be a high school teacher and that I did not want to incur the out-of-state tuition that Hampton and Howard University charged. Since these two were the only other schools that I had considered, that left North Carolina College at Durham as my final destination. As it turned out, that was a very good choice for me to have made. Richard, Bernice, Laquitta, Depriest Beverly and Sherman Perry also selected NCC, so I knew at least someone to talk with upon my arrival.

Upon arrival at NCC, I was assigned a room in McLean Hall. The room was about twelve feet square, and I was given three roommates; Floyd Harvey, James Blackwell and Jimmy Mullins. We had double-deck bunk beds, and I chose the top bed over James Blackwell. Each of my roommates had his own set of peculiarities. Each was likable in certain ways, and each presented an adjustment for me in certain other ways.

Floyd Harvey took charge of the housekeeping right away. He established rules that the rest of us followed. Pick up your things and put them away. Study your homework before playing cards. Don't smoke in bed. Floyd would take our money if we had any and then give it back to us in portions that he decided we needed. He was our mother away from home. Funny thing about that is that Floyd was the smallest and the physically weakest among us. We gave him that power over us because he won our trust.

Jimmy Mullins was from Brooklyn and he epitomized the stereotype that I had of the city slicker. He ran track, and I was sure that he had learned to run to escape the police. Jimmy was a serious student and a good friend. He was easily distracted by the ladies, and this fact led to some problems for him down the road.

James Blackwell was from Weldon, North Carolina. Sometimes, he claimed to have been from Enfield, so I associate him with both those places. It was common in those days for people to lie about where they were from, so I never put much stock in what was said along those lines. In any case, James enjoyed his freshman year as much as was humanly possible. He left us shortly thereafter, and I did not see him again until sometimes in the late eighties.

My freshman year was one of challenging adjustments for me. I had to learn to study and to use the library. I had to learn the politics of college life, how to write term papers the way professors wanted them written, how to never appear to have some information that you had learned somewhere other than in that particular teacher's classroom. The pace of college was much different than that of high school in that there were no bells ringing to tell you when to go here or there. There was no uniform schedule for all students, so learning my classmates was more difficult than I had imagined that it would be.

I managed to get through my freshman year, but my academic record was one of which even I was amazed. Had that been high school, I would not have wanted to take my report card home. I had made "A"s in all the subjects that I liked and under the teachers whose teaching style I enjoyed. In my other classes, I had made "C"s and

"D"s. Mr. Holmes, my Spanish teacher, in whose class I made my first "D", continually reminded me that I did not belong in college. By the second quarter of my sophomore year, I had concluded that he was right, so I left school and volunteered for the United States Marine Corps.

My stay in the Marine Corps was abbreviated by the discovery that the heart murmur that had ended my football career in high school had returned. The Marine Corps gave me an assurance that when I got healthy, they would take me back, but after I left, I never heard from them again. That brief experience was a turning point in my life. I had seen enough to appreciate the opportunity that going to school had been, and I returned to college more determined to apply my ability to the task at hand. For the first time, I became a good student, winning the respect of my teachers and of my peers. In my first month back in school, I was elected to serve on the Student Government. In my junior year I was elected to serve as class president and was re-elected to that same position in my senior year.

In spite of having missed a quarter of a school year, I went on to graduate with my entering class. I did so by attending summer school and by carrying a full load of courses over the rest of my college career. The realization of how near I had come to missing the grand experience of college made me a better student and a better person. It caused me to focus on the blessings that were mine rather than on the difficulties and inconveniences that are a predictable part of life for all of us.

MY FATHER - William W. Flood

FLOOD FAMILY

Back row - left to right: Dudley, Ashley, Josephine, James, Henry

Front row - left to right: Beatrice, Nancy, Mother, Minnie, Virginia

**BARBARA & DUDLEY'S
FIRST DATE
April 1953**

OUR WEDDING DAY - November 22, 1956

**BARBARA & DUDLEY'S
FIFTIETH WEDDING ANNIVERSARY**

My First Real Romance

As I have related before, I got off to a late start in the area of romance. When I arrived at college, I was not the least bit interested in having a steady girlfriend. During my freshman and sophomore years, I met many girls and even dated a few of them, but never managed to develop a serious relationship with any of them. By my junior year, I had regained my old high school status of being every girl's friend, but nobody's soul mate.

One of my closest friends, Charles Asbury, was in the same sad position. All the girls liked Charles, but he had no special girlfriend. I wondered why. After all, Charles was handsome, intelligent, witty, neat and well dressed, and was well spoken. Yet, he had no special lady like most of the other fellows.

One of the student functions at NCC was the Annual Sweetheart Ball. This was a dress occasion on which the ladies donned their long evening gowns and the guys wore their rented white dinner jackets and dark pants. It was held on campus in the gym, so there was little reason not to attend unless you could not get a date to take to the dance. Neither Charles nor I had made plans to attend and we frequently kidded each other about having no one to escort.

During one lunch period while we were standing in the usual long and slow moving line in the dining hall, Charles pointed out to me a young lady that he had decided to ask to the dance. Her name was Barbara Thomas. He had not spoken to her about it, but he was certain she would say "yes" to his invitation. I told Charles that I doubted that she would accept his invitation, to which he responded, "five dollars says she will." My response was "that's a bet." I didn't know Barbara Thomas from Adam's house cat, and I wondered why I had allowed myself to be dragged into a bet of that sort. I felt sure that Charles Asbury could have had his pick from among the ladies at NCC, and furthermore, I didn't have five dollars to my name.

As the line moved past the water fountain, I decided to take a drink of water to remove some of the choking feeling from my throat. When I raised my head from the fountain, there behind me stood Barbara Thomas. She formerly introduced herself to me and asked if I would like to accompany her to the Sweetheart Ball. I nearly dropped my teeth. My first thought was that this would clinch my bet with Asbury, but on further reflection, I thought that I might actually enjoy her company for an evening, so I accepted. Asbury never paid me the five dollars. Even worse, I later learned that Barbara's girlfriends had bet her that she would not be able to get a date with me.

Barbara and I attended the dance along with Charles Asbury, Jim Nate Felton and Chuck Staton, all of whom got as many dances as I did. When the dance ended, Charles and I walked Barbara back to her dorm. She and I did agree to talk again. As time went on, Barbara and I became the best of friends. She was an exceptionally talented student of music, an area that was a major part of my life. Barbara had the most delicate touch on the piano keyboard that I had ever heard, but for reasons unknown to me, she was very lacking in confidence.

I appointed myself as the person who would build confidence in Barbara by promoting her self-esteem and lessening her need for external affirmation. Little did I know that fifty-five years later, I would still be working with her on these same issues. Though she made great strides, she never fully achieved either of these objectives.

Barbara was a multi-talented, complex person. She was an accomplished seamstress and could have had a career in that area had she so chosen. She could knit and cook, and she was an immaculate housekeeper. She was good at conversation and she met people easily. She dressed flawlessly, and she laughed freely. She was fiercely loyal to her family. I found in Barbara a lot of commonality with my most cherished values.

Having dated Barbara for nearly four years, I asked her one night at a gasoline station after having filled my car with the cheapest gas available if she would marry me. She seemed surprised that I had asked and I was equally surprised that she accepted. On November 22,1956, we exchanged vows with her sister, Anne, serving as bridesmaid and my brother, James, standing as my best man.

Barbara and I were, at the time of our marriage, working in two separate locations. She was employed as a teacher in Gaston County, North Carolina, and I was teaching and coaching in Hertford County in Eastern North Carolina in the very school that I had attended. The driving time between her residence and mine was six hours each way. Typically, we would meet on weekends at her mother's home in Burlington which was roughly half-way. After a year of this arrangement, we decided that we needed to live in the same town even if only one of us had employment. So, in her usual cooperative manner, Barbara agreed to move to my home in Winton. We lived there for the next ten years before relocating to Greenville, North Carolina where we lived for three years. On January 1, 1970, we moved to Raleigh, North Carolina where we resided until Barbara's death on March 20, 2012. Of all our wonderful experiences, the memory of having lived in Winton stood out in Barbara's mind as the most pleasant times that we ever enjoyed.

In 1957, as previously referenced, Barbara and I built our first house. We had very little money, so we purchased a package from a company that would erect a "shell" which consisted of the exterior of a house. The owner would finish the inside.

Barbara and I did the sheet rock, the floors, the ceilings and the painting. In addition, Barbara made the drapery and I built the cabinets. To my pride, that house is still standing today.

Coming Back to Winton

After graduating from NCC, my plan was to go to California with "Bookie" Turner and Richard Gadsden, take the civil service exam, make a high score on it, and get a high paying job in the post office. I fell two or three days short of executing that plan when Richard received a call from Mr. Freeland offering him a teaching position at C. S. Brown. Richard accepted the offer and went home to teach. "Bookie" went on to California where he still resides. I remained in Atlantic City, New Jersey for the next several months, waiting tables at Frailinger's, learning about life from Calvin Weeks who had lived on the "sorry side" of town, and taking note of all the things I did not want to do with my life. After living through a hurricane and a hard freeze in early fall, I concluded that the sunny climate of North Carolina was to be my destination. So, I came back to NCC and took some courses to prepare me for a teaching career. The following year, I came back home to Winton as a teacher at "dear old CSB".

It was September of 1955, and I was the new kid on the block in my own hometown and my own school. I had seen the school from the perspective of a student, but now the view was very different. I had walked the streets and frequented the local haunts as a child, but now that instant manhood had been thrust upon me, I was both excited and afraid.

I was assigned to teach eighth grade math, language and physical education. In my class were several students who were near my age and certainly thought of themselves as being adults. There were others who had not matured even to the level of their chronological age of fourteen. In that setting, I was to learn a lot about human sociology.

In addition to my teaching duties, I was assigned to the position of assistant football coach. Mr. Varner was still the head coach at that time, and he made it clear that he didn't want much assistance. His annual message to the team, and I suspected to the assistant coaches as well, had not changed since I had played on his team; "football is a game of co-operation: if you will 'co', I will 'operate'"; and "operate" he did. My role was to get the players into game condition, so I led the exercise drills and pre-game warm-ups. Beyond that, I gave individual advice to any player who came to me in private, but when the game was being played, I "co"ed and Mr. Varner "operated".

One division of the eighth grade consisted almost entirely of children from my neighborhood. These children and I would interact on many levels during that year. I had grown up with their older siblings and I knew their parents well. They played in my yard after school and on weekends. They rode with me to see college games at Elizabeth City State College. For most of them, I became more of a parent than a teacher.

My tenure at C. S. Brown was short. At the end of the first year, the school lost a teaching position due to declining enrollment, and since I had been the last teacher to be hired, it was my position that was to be vacated. At the same time that I received this news, I was told that Riverview Elementary School in Murfreesboro had gained a position and that Mr. Abner Bowe, the principal, was interested in having me to come there to teach. I did not know Mr. Bowe, but I knew his wife who had been my sister Minnie's classmate and who was now working in the central office of the school system. I reasoned that because he was married to Geneva, Mr. Bowe had to be all right, so I applied for the job and was hired.

Going to Riverview meant that I would not have to relocate since it was only nine miles from my house. Further, Mr. Freeland had told me that if he ever regained the position that he had lost, he hoped that I would consider coming back to C. S. Brown. My interest in the Winton area had been re-kindled to the point that leaving the system was not a viable option for me, so I was eager to accept Mr. Bowe's offer. Little did I know at the time that the Riverview experience would establish a direction that would lead me toward the principalship and ultimately toward an expanded career at the state level in education.

Mr. Bowe invited me to come to the school for an interview in early June. During that interview, he made his intentions very clear to me. He said that he had an excellent staff of teachers, all of whom were women, and that he did not need a teacher as much as he needed a male who would work with the male students in their development toward manhood. He assured me that while I would be assigned some teaching duties, a lot of my work would be done outside the classroom. He asked me to begin by establishing a Boy Scout troop at the school and to build an outdoor basketball court in preparation for starting a team for the sixth, seventh and eighth grade students.

I liked Mr. Bowe right away. He assigned me to teach all the science in all the grades, one through eight. I had no classroom of my own, but I was the only teacher that had an office. I kept my portable lab and my plant and animal collection in the office. I also used it as a place to counsel some of the students who needed special attention. My schedule directed that I teach science in each of the primary classrooms once a week, the fourth, fifth and sixth, twice a week, and the seventh and eighth, three times a week. Between my visits, the regular classroom teacher was expected to carry on the science instruction.

During the first of my years at Riverview, I learned the names and families of most of the students. Through my Boy Scout work, my coaching of the teams, and my civic work in the community, I become more knowledgeable of the conditions under which our students had to prepare for their respective futures. I went into every neighborhood represented in the school, and I talked to anyone who would talk with me about the children. I visited their churches and their hangouts. I made it known that if you miss school without a valid reason, I will find out about it and will come after you.

The teachers at Riverview were a fairly close-knit group. They accepted me into their culture immediately, so I had no adjustment period to endure. After a few days, I felt as if I had been there forever. Many times, I had to ask one of the regular classroom teachers to cover my subject matter while I completed some non-class assignment that Mr. Bowe had given me. They all seemed willing to help me in that way. Mrs. Gladys Lawrence, one of my many mentors, had never liked the idea of someone else instructing her students even for two periods a week, so I tried as best I could to make hers the class that I would miss when other things took me away.

Being the only male teacher had its blessings and its challenges. The male students that were in need of male influence sought me out for discussions that were not characteristically a part of the student-teacher relationship during that era. They talked to me about schoolwork, family matters and about their personal lives. As the word got around that I would listen to their issues, the girl students began to confide in me as well. We had no guidance counselor in the school, so for many of our students, I executed that function. For some others, I was the dean of discipline and the interrupter of their plans to be idle. The smaller children in the lower grades would run up to me wanting to be picked up and hugged. The eighth grade girls wanted to know about my personal life, whether I was dating, why didn't I have a wife and what I did in my time away from school. Fortunately, my life was non-controversial and I had nothing to hide from them, so we had some very frank discussions about life and about creating one's own paths to success. Many of the students that I taught in that first year have kept in contact with me ever since, and I have been made proud by the achievements of many of them.

The Inimitable Landon Miales

During my second year at Riverview, Mr. Bowe hired a substitute teacher from Gates County whose name was Landon Miales. Landon was a recent graduate of Elizabeth City State College who had served in the United States Armed Forces, so he brought a little more than the new teacher level of maturity when he came to us. Landon appeared to be quiet and even shy until he got to know the people around him. After that, he was quite friendly and outgoing.

Landon and I became instant friends. We shared the same background with respect to our upbringing. He had been the only male child in his family and felt a great sense of responsibility for his mother and sisters. Though I had brothers, I felt that same responsibility, and we often talked about what that meant to us. Landon liked sports and he enjoyed yard work. He was good at building things and painting. He liked raising a garden. More important than any of these things was the fact that he was fiercely loyal to his friends. He had the unusual ability to make your pain less painful and your joys more enjoyable. His sense of humor was his trademark and he never made someone else the brunt of the joke.

After the first semester of his year at Riverview, Landon took a full time teaching job at Amanda S. Cherry School in Harrelsville, North Carolina. Now he would have an additional few miles to drive to work every day, but this seemed not to faze him at all. Each day on the way from school, he would stop by our house, or during football season when I was on the field after school, he would stop by practice and stay until it was over. Then we would spend a few minutes talking about nothing important and laughing about how serious other people seemed to be about things that mattered little to us. It was rare for a day to pass that we did not visit each other, if only by phone.

After a few years at Amanda S. Cherry, Miales was promoted to principal of the school. At that time, it was the custom that principals had very little association on a social level with teachers. Yet, there was no change in our friendship because of his promotion. Neither was there any change in the things that we had always done together. We painted houses during the summer months to supplement our modest teaching salaries, and this continued after his promotion.

We also worked with the maintenance crew that painted our school buildings during the summer. Mr. Dixon, our supervisor was very pleased to have a principal on his summer team. By that time neither of us was working for the money, but rather we were working for the pleasure we found in improving our schools and in the fellowship within the work crew.

When I decided to leave the county, the greatest support that I received for making the transition came from Landon Miales. He gave me the assurance that I would be able to handle the principalship of a school. He even offered his help, were I to need it, in getting things organized and running smoothly. I didn't take him up on the offer, but it was comforting to know that such support was available to me.

When I was asked to come to work at Bethel Union School as assistant principal, and when I suddenly found myself cast into the role of principal, the first thing I did was to call Landon Miales and offer him the job as my assistant. The job would have paid him more than he was then earning, and most assuredly, would have placed him in position for a principalship in a much larger school within a short period of time. Landon declined my offer because of his dedication to the job that he was currently holding and to the community which he was currently serving. I respected that decision.

Several years later, when I had been hired to work with the effort to desegregate the public schools of North Carolina, I again offered Landon a job that he also declined. I did not elaborate on that particular job to him because it would have been unfair to him to have done so. At that time, my job placed me at risk every day, and I felt that if I were to be in danger of losing my life, the one person that I would have wanted to be covering my back was Landon Miales. Had he known of the danger that I regularly faced, he would have taken the job without regard to the personal sacrifice it would have been for him. Such was the friendship that we shared.

More than fifty years have passed since Landon and I first met through the coincidence of working together in the Hertford County Schools. While that seems like a long time in some respects, little has changed about our friendship over those years. We do not visit or talk to each other on a regular basis as we once did, but whenever we are in the same place, we begin wherever we left off last time.

Returning to C. S. Brown

After eight very special years at Riverview School, I was again reunited with my alma mater, C. S. Brown. This time, I was hired to teach in the high school and to coach the girls' basketball team. I was also assigned duties as the assistant football coach and as assistant to Mr. Mayo, the head coach of the boys' basketball team.

Returning to C. S. Brown required no effort on my part. While at Riverview, I had continued to work with the teams at Brown in an informal capacity, so I already knew the students. Many of the high school students had been in my classes at Riverview, and many of the others had seen me at games or in the community. The transition went smoothly for me. My initial teaching area for which I had studied at NCC was social studies, and I was now using that knowledge for the first time after nine years of teaching.

Coaching the girls' basketball team was a real pleasure for me. We were fairly successful that first year. I explained to the girls who came out for basketball that we intended to build a championship team within three years. My plan for doing so would require that we focus on players from grades nine and ten so as to develop a team of experienced players within two years. I told them that I would keep no juniors and seniors that were not on the starting team. As it turned out, only one senior remained on the team. That senior was my niece, Trinette Burford who had grown up in our home and who had imitated my brother James and me in everything we did, including playing basketball in our backyard. "Trin" was the tallest girl who came out, and was the most coachable of the lot. Her becoming a starter had nothing to do with her being my niece, though I am sure that some who were not starting made that assumption.

In our second season, we were a pretty good team. "Trin" had graduated, and several of the younger players had become more aware of the fundamentals of the game. We had developed a system that involved some rigorous defense and a passing game that set up some easy baskets inside the lane. We had some athletic girls with high energy levels who were not reluctant to dive on the floor after loose balls and to box out the opponents under both baskets. A couple of them were good ball handlers and we had about three excellent outside shooters. We had learned to play as a team rather than as a group of individuals.

This team went on to post the best winning record of any girls' basketball team in the history of the school. More importantly, every one of our starters except Gloria Fallice would be returning for the next year. Diane Smith had become a complete player, handling the ball with confidence. Joan "Beefy" Lewis, so named because she used her body so well to block out and to take it to the hoop, had learned to pace herself and to play within her skills. Darlene Porter had learned to gather herself before shooting the ball and to keep the ball up over her head so as to capitalize on her considerable height. Maggie Archer had developed a deadly outside shot. Shirley Weaver had become a stopper on defense. Margaret Chavis had learned to play with her back to the basket. The Watford sisters had developed well although Shirley was not fully committed to playing basketball. Maria Felton could shoot the ball well and had improved on her shot selection. Several of my former

Murfreesboro students were ready to step in and make a contribution. We seemed headed for a very good season.

That season was not to be. Before the season was to begin, I received the news that C. S. Brown would no longer field a girls' basketball team. The reason was that some of the women teachers resented having to serve as escorts when the team practiced and played its games. The year was 1966, and the atmosphere was such that at our school, a male teacher could not hold practice for the girls' team without a woman being present. During the first two years that I had coached the team, my wife had come to practice whenever I was not able to get a female faculty member to stay. But after two years of hearing complaints, Mr. Freeland had lost the will to require teachers to serve as chaperones, and he lacked the courage to entrust the job of monitoring the team to just the male coaches. As a result, we lost our chance at developing a great program for girls at our school.

I went on to become the assistant to Mr. Mayo, the boys' basketball coach, but I continued to be disappointed that the girls' team had been discontinued. Our girls had worked so very hard to become a good team and several of them were on the verge of becoming exceptional players. Connie Brown, one of our best players, had already transferred to Ahoskie High School where she went on to have an outstanding career on the court. For most of the other girls, transfer was not a realistic option, so all their hard work went unrewarded. Though Mr. Mayo and I were the best of friends, I knew that the basketball team was his, not mine, and I felt a great loss when that change was made.

All the coaches at C. S. Brown were in one way or another involved with both football and basketball-the only two sports in which the school participated. By the time of my return to C. S. Brown, Mr. Turner Coggins had been named head football coach. While teaching at Riverview School, I had continued to work informally with Coach Varner, and later, Coach Cooper when they had each served as head football coach. Coach Coggins had a different approach to working together than is generally found on a football team. He viewed all the coaches as equal partners, and he openly deferred to anyone on the staff who had an idea or a suggestion for improving any aspect of the program. Turner and I became close friends and we remained so even after our coaching days were over.

Though my work at and with the schools was very gratifying, there was another element of our time in Winton that for me is unforgettable. The young men who Barbara always referred to as "Dudley's Boys" were very special. Our interaction with them fostered their growth and ours.

Winton had no organized activities for local youth outside the school and their respective churches. Most of the local boys spent their leisure time engaged in unproductive activity. Having grown up in Winton, I was acutely aware of the lack of opportunity for the development of young black men, so I was motivated to broaden these opportunities in any small way that I could. Hence, our home became a virtual community center for the local boys and some of the local girls.

Prior to our having built our own house, Barbara and I, along with my sister, Nancy and her two sons, lived in the house that was formerly owned by the founder of our school, Dr. C. S. Brown. It was quite a stately house surrounded by a very large yard with a large pecan tree on the property and space for a large vegetable garden. This arrangement allowed us to set up a basketball goal, a badminton court, a horse shoe pit, a croquet court and a ping pong table. Next to the property was a vacant lot owned by the school that allowed us to play touch football. Three blocks from us was an excellent baseball diamond which we used whenever the local "semi-pro" teams were not playing. When Barbara and I built our own house, we made certain that we had enough space to continue all of these activities with the youth.

Barbara and I owned the only house with central heat and air that most of these youth had ever experienced. We also owned the only color television set to which they had access. Every day after school and every weekend, our house and yard was filled with the local boys. On most Saturdays, some of us would go fishing in the Chowan River in the early morning. By noon, we would have caught enough fish to feed the group that would assemble for the weekly fish fry in our backyard. The scent of frying fish was sure to draw a crowd which sometimes included passersby that we may or may not even know. We nearly always caught enough fish to accommodate whoever came to join us. After the fish were consumed, the games would begin and would last until darkness overtook us.

On Saturdays when there would be a football or basketball game at Elizabeth City State College, Barbara and I would take a car loaded with boys to the game. On some occasions, there were so many wanting to go to the games or to the beach that each of us would drive taking a load. We would generally pay their admission fees to these activities and buy them food and sodas of their choosing. In return, they would help us with odd jobs around our house, most of which were created just to give them the feeling of carrying their own weight.

The boys treated us as if we were their parents. They were particularly respectful to Barbara and she was very fond of all of them. Barbara, not being a native of Winton, was amused to learn that hardly anyone there was known by his given name. Some had "nick names" that were so emblazoned that even now, I have trouble remembering their given names. Among them were my brother James "Pic" Flood; Calvin "Boo" Williams; Johnny "Pancho" Vann; Ronnie "Eyes" Vann; Lindwood "Bugs" Harrison; Louis "Lippy" Harrison; Leon "Monkey" Britt; James Arthur "Bootie" Majette; Horace "Candy Ball" Archer; Roger "Sugar" Archer; Louis "Smoke" Britt; Gerald "Skeeter" Manley; John "Bro" Britt;

John "Bootsie" Jarrett; Lawrence "Coon" Jarrett; Charles "Neighbor" Jarrett and Larry "Louse" Archer. There were others, all of whom had a tag that had been given them by their peers. This was their way of saying that we were all family.

All of our "boys" loved sports and most of them excelled at one or more sports. The Archer boys were golfers and each could also play basketball. The Jarrett boys were good at football and basketball. The Vann boys were good baseball players. James Flood and Calvin Williams were good at all sports. My brother, James could throw a football accurately for 60 yards when he was in high school. Vernon Watford could catch a pass 60 yards down field on a fairly regular basis.

The Decision to Leave Winton

While living in Winton, I was very active in the affairs of First Baptist Church Winton. I taught the adult Sunday School class, sang in two choirs, and along with my wife, Barbara, worked with the youth department of the church. I was also the church clerk.

Over a period of two or three years, we had several preachers to serve our church who did not stay around very long for one reason or another. The last preacher to serve while we were still in Winton was the person responsible for my leaving the area. He was the Rev. John H. Taylor from Greenville, North Carolina. Rev. Taylor was the coordinator for Title I programs in the Pitt County Schools, and was one of only two Black central office administrators in that school system at that time. Almost from the day we met, he used his considerable influence to prompt me to see myself as a potential educational leader.

Prior to my association with John Taylor, my greatest ambition had been to someday serve as a principal in one of the Hertford County Schools. Before the schools were integrated, the possibility of that happening was remote, because Black principals never gave up their schools for any reason short of death. Still, I was content to wait my turn. Mr. R. P. Martin, the Superintendent of Hertford County Schools, had told me that he had plans to move me into a significant leadership position, but he could not give me a definite timetable. So at the urging of John Taylor, I accepted a position as assistant principal for Bethel Union School in Pitt County.

The move to Pitt County was easier than I had imagined that it would be. The county also hired Barbara, my wife, to serve as music supervisor for the school district. Though I had not previously held the title of assistant principal, I had filled that role for Mr. Bowe while teaching at Riverview School. So, I felt confident that I was up to the task at hand. Had I known what was just ahead, I may have been a little less confident.

I reported to my new job on July 1, 1967. I spent the better part of the first day riding around the county with Mr. Arthur Alford, the county superintendent of schools. Mr. Alford told me that Mr. Elliot, the current principal of Bethel Union School would be retiring at the end of that school year, and that I would then become the principal of that school. This seemed to me to be too short a time to prepare to take the helm of a school of 1,288 students in grades one through twelve. John Taylor, Barbara and my friend Landon Miales, who was already serving as principal, convinced me that I was ready for the challenge. Even they could not have foreseen the events that would occur over that summer.

On August 1, 1967, we received the directive that the Pitt County Schools would begin the serious business of desegregating its schools immediately. The plan for doing so would require the reassignment of 288 students to Bethel Union that had previously attended elsewhere, and the relocation of five White teachers to Bethel Union. This was to be achieved in time for an opening date of August 15th for teachers, and for the last Monday in August for students. On August 11th, Mr. Elliot made the decision to retire immediately, and I was named principal.

I had no time to be afraid or to feel sorry for myself. We had a school to open, students to locate, bus routes to plan, new teachers to orient, parents to meet, churches to visit and a community to win over to our point of view about what its school should and could become. We had no time to waste, so I went right to work on those matters. By the time the students came, our school was ready for them. It was only then that I had the time to panic over the whole situation in which I found myself. After the first week for students, I sat down with Barbara and shared with her that I was not cut out to be a school principal, and that I intended to tender my resignation at the end of the month. She prevailed upon me to give it until Thanksgiving before making a final decision. I took her advice, and by Thanksgiving, I had fallen in love with Bethel Union School.

At Bethel, I was blessed to have a supportive faculty and staff. Many of them admired my drive and my advocacy for the students. The students had been badly short-changed for years, and I was determined to modify that situation. I spoke out for the needs of the school, and we began to be taken seriously by those who made decisions that determined our fate. The morale of the teachers rose to a level that they really enjoyed teaching at Bethel Union. The students began to take their education seriously. Discipline was greatly improved in the school. New teachers coming into the school were made to feel a part of its fabric right away. I felt fortunate to be in a place where my every effort seemed to make a great positive impact.

Upon my arrival at Bethel, I was reunited with one of my schoolmates from North Carolina College. That person was Marian Winslow Jones. I had known Marian at NCC as the "homey" of my running buddy, James Nate Felton. She was the first teacher to approach me upon my arrival and to pledge her support even when I was the assistant principal. When I became principal, I asked her to help me to put the finances of the school in order since her major field was business. Within two years, Marian led us from being deeply in debt to fiscal soundness. For that I am deeply grateful.

Pencie Nixon was the guidance counselor when I arrived at Bethel Union. She had such great rapport with children that I considered making her an assistant principal, but then I realized that she was more valuable to the school in the role she was already occupying. I relied heavily on her experience with the community and on her knowledge of education. I made no important decision without first discussing it with Miss Nixon.

Bernard Haselrig came to Bethel as my assistant at the beginning of my second year. I had recruited Bernard because of the rapport he had evidenced in his basketball-coaching career. I had observed his gentle but firm approach to working with young men, and we needed that influence at our school. He came in on blind faith, not knowing me except by reputation, and we immediately became a team. There was no distinction in the minds of the students as to who was in charge. They all loved and respected Mr. Haselrig. His being there was the reason that I felt comfortable to leave and take a position at the North Carolina Department of Public Instruction at the end of 1969. Bernard followed me as principal and remained there until the school was consolidated into North Pitt as a part of the desegregation plan.

While I was serving as principal at Bethel Union, I became very active in the affairs of the community in and around Bethel and Greenville.

Desegregation of the races was arriving slowly and painfully for most of the people that I made friends with. It came much more naturally for me because I had never held to the idea that people should be separated along the lines of race or class. I was appointed to the Good Neighbor Council, a group that worked to bring the races together in harmony. Within a month after that appointment, I was named co-chairman of the Council. In that capacity, I was invited to speak to groups all over the county, many of which had never had a Black speaker before. I was well received by every group to which I spoke. Many of the White and Black churches had me to come as their Laymen's Day speaker.

Soon, I began receiving invitations to speak on racial matters to groups outside my living area. I was forced to expand my own understanding of the issues around race relations since I had been thrust into the position to publicly teach about such matters. I began to read anything that I could find on the subject of human relations and to attend workshops and lectures on that subject at every possible opportunity. I took a course in race relations at East Carolina University, and I took other courses in sociology and political science so as to upgrade my knowledge of human behavior. More importantly than anything else, I allowed myself to have firsthand interaction with as many people from as many different backgrounds as I possibly could. In a short time, I began to be recognized as a person with some unusual ability to work with human problems and to further good human relations.

In January 1969, I received a phone call from the newly elected State Superintendent of Public Instruction asking if I would consider serving on the State Textbook Committee. This was a heretofore all White committee that previewed all curricular materials presented for use in the schools of North Carolina and made recommendations to the State Board of Education as to which of these materials to adopt and purchase. The Governor, usually on the recommendation of the State Superintendent, made appointments to this committee. After some deliberation, I accepted that appointment, and working in that environment, I got to know the State Superintendent, A. Craig Phillips, quite well.

From the first exposure that I had to Craig Phillips, I saw in him something that I had never before detected in a public official except the

Mayor of Winton, Mr. J. R. Jordan. He was open and outgoing, warm and pleasant, wise and willing to learn, forceful and gentle, demanding and nurturing. He forced me to re-evaluate my thinking about public officials. Based on my experiences up until that time, my impressions of public officials was less than complimentary. It was refreshing to learn that there was at least one person in a high office who genuinely cared about people.

Soon after Craig Phillips took office, he established it as a priority to dismantle the dual school system in North Carolina. To achieve this objective, he established a technical assistance unit within the Department of Public Instruction, which he named the Division of Human Relations. He hired Robert Ed Strother, the Superintendent of Greene County Schools, to lead that effort. He initially added to the team Gene Causby, a junior high principal from Goldsboro, and Harold Webb, a consultant in the Department of Public Instruction for many years. In November of 1969, I was asked to come to the Department to become a part of that division. Harold Webb was promoted to become the director of Title I programs, and I was to replace him on the desegregation team. I accepted the offer and began working informally with the team from that time on until I could be released from my duties at Bethel Union School. In January 1970, I became a full-time member of the Division of Human Relations.

On the day that I arrived to begin work at the State Department of Public Instruction, I was informed that a serious situation was underway in Hyde County, and that my priority would be to work with that situation until it was resolved. Gene Causby and I set out for Hyde County even before I had located a permanent home in Raleigh. Since we still had our home in Greenville, it was convenient for me to work from there for a short while. However, the unrest in Hyde County eventually led to a year-long boycott of the school system. Other school systems were experiencing similar problems that claimed our attention. In March of that year, our move to Raleigh was completed, but I continued to work in Hyde County for most of the rest of that year.

The issue in Hyde County arose over the decision by the school board to close the O. A. Peay School in Swan Quarter, or to continue its existence in some form other than a senior high school. This decision did not meet the approval of the Black community, and in protest of the decision, many of the Black parents kept their children home from school. Meanwhile, hostility was growing among the adults. Soon, episodes of violence occurred, and though there was no loss of life, the relations between the races reached a dangerously low point.

There were marches in Hyde County and marches from Hyde County to Raleigh organized by persons who were trying to call attention to what they believed to be an unjust decision. The O. A. Peay School had long been the heartbeat of the Black community, and it represented much more than merely a place to hold school. It was the cultural center, the political force, and the meeting place for all the activities that involved Blacks from all walks of life. The only other sites on which Blacks regularly gathered were the churches, but no one church served the total community. Only the school held that distinction. Even before the decision was finalized concerning the fate of O. A. Peay School, resistance had begun to build against any change that might diminish its role in the community. Local citizens had contacted Golden Frinks, an activist and civic leader from Edenton. Golden had ties to the Southern Christian Leadership Conference that had been founded by the Rev. Dr. Martin Luther King, Jr., and through his efforts, the Hyde County situation received national attention. When the issue was resolved, such attention had been given to the matter that other leaders in other communities took note of the methods that had been employed in Hyde County, and this cycle was to be replicated many times in the years just ahead.

The Hyde County dispute provided me with a lot of insight into the manner that civil disruption can work in a community. When we were called to work in other such situations, we always used the lessons that we had learned in Hyde County to help to bring about just and reasonable solutions. Among the things we learned was the fact that when people are faced with having to make a major change in the way they are accustomed to relating to their fellow humans, it either brings out the best in them or the worst in them. More often, it is the latter. It became clear to me that the idea of sharing power with persons who had been seen as not having a leadership role in our society was very offensive to those who were accustomed to being in power. In North Carolina, this issue was complicated by the fact that Whites were, and had always been, in power. Blacks were beginning to demand that they be included in the decision making process, so every power struggle became a racial issue as well.

Over the next three years, Gene Causby and I would work with civil disruption in virtually every school district in North Carolina. Some disruptions were minor–involving such things as a student walkout in protest of some board of education policy or an administrative decision that was unpopular. Others had a major impact on their respective communities. At least one county experienced such disunity that it petitioned the General Assembly to allow it to divide into two separate counties.

Student unrest was an everyday occurrence, and parents were always involved in these situations, though many times their involvement was behind the scene. In many of these situations, we were able to serve as mediators between opposing forces. In others, the feelings were so tense that local people were unable to sit in the same room and talk through an issue with a person for whom they had no respect. In such cases, we served as go-betweens, taking messages from one group to the other until an accord could be reached that would allow them to sit together. Still other situations were so tense that violence was inevitable. These situations were generally characterized by there being well-established advantages that some group was enjoying, and these advantages being threatened by some other group. I learned that when people are accustomed to having certain privileges, they come to view them as rights, and they will fight to the death to protect that which they have determined to be their rights. People of privilege see no meaningful distinction between their wants and their needs. Their sense of self-worth enables them to heap injustices upon the weak and to convince themselves that the less fortunate persons really bring their state of affairs upon themselves.

During the three-year period between 1969 and 1972, North Carolina made great strides in race relations. The desegregation of the public schools led to further opportunities for people who had been separated by legal and social doctrine to experience meaningful interaction for the first time. Obviously, not everyone moved at the same pace in the matter of improving relations between races. Many persons of color had experienced treatment at the hands of their White counterparts that made it impossible for them to trust the new acceptance that was being extended to them. Many Whites' racial attitudes were so deeply ingrained that they were not able or willing to view any Black as their equal. These attitudes were particularly problematic in the various workplaces in which the races were forced by circumstance to work as peers.

In June 1975, I was promoted to the position of Assistant State Superintendent for Human Relations and Student Affairs. In this position, I was to change my focus from putting out the fires of school disruption to that of building meaningful programs that would lead to improved relations among the various factions that made up our public school community. Gene Causby was promoted to the position of Assistant State Superintendent for Personnel Relations and Public Affairs at the same time of my promotion, so I was losing the most effective partner that I had ever had in working on human relations problems. I will say more about that relationship later in this book, but the notion of tackling the challenge ahead without the immediate and daily help of Gene was unattractive to say the least. Craig Phillips made it clear that it was not his intention to break up the most successful team that this state had produced, but that each of us had earned a promotion. Furthermore, he made it clear that he was relying on our good sense to utilize the strength of our relationship to keep the momentum toward a more civil society alive. This we were able to do.

As the climate began to change, and improved relationships between the races began to be a priority for more school administrators across the nation, Gene and I began receiving requests for our services from all around the country. By the end of the year 1975, we had worked together in more than half the states in this country presenting solutions to racial problems. We had worked with every conceivable population in our society, ranging from social organizations to public school students, boards of education, teachers, administrators and parents. We had worked with disruptive issues and with school re-districting and student re-assignment issues. We had developed strategies for reducing student unrest in the schools and for providing greater and more meaningful student involvement in the decision making process. We had helped to change the way that school people saw each other across racial lines, and we had given them new concepts of how far mutual respect could take them toward having better schools and a better society. While doing these things, we modeled all that we taught through the relationship that we had developed. There was no way of mistaking the fact that we were genuine friends, thus proving that persons from different racial and ethnic backgrounds could work and live together in harmony.

In the early days of our teaming, Gene and I learned anew how deep the prejudices held by some people reached into their very souls. When we traveled, we always shared a room at whatever hotel or motel at which we would stay. On one occasion, we had traveled to Cincinnati, Ohio for a speaking engagement. Upon arrival at the hotel, we asked for the double accommodation room that we had reserved and for which we were holding a written confirmation. We were told by the desk clerk that no double room was available and that she would have to give us each a single room. We complained that to do so would increase the cost to us since sharing a room was much less expensive than having a room each. The desk clerk agreed that she would give us the two separate rooms for the cost of one double. Upon reaching our rooms, we found that she had given us each a double room. Without any discussion, we moved our things into one of the rooms and slept in the other.

On a trip to Jackson, Mississippi, Gene and I flew into the Jackson airport and rented a car to drive over to our hotel. Prior to this particular trip, I had injured my knee while working in my yard, and I was using a cane to aid me in walking. When we arrived at the hotel, Gene took both our luggage from the car to the front desk. The hotel lobby was filled with White men who had never seen a White man carrying the luggage of a Black man. Thinking this might be a good learning experience for them, I turned to Gene and said, "Come on, boy." There was enough tension in the air that you could physically feel it as they checked us into our shared room.

On another occasion, we were spending a Sunday night in a motel in Chester, South Carolina. There was only one eating place within miles of the motel, so we decided to have dinner there. When we entered, the place was filled with people who were waiting to be served. However, we were seated immediately, served at once, and our check came to us with the food. One may have concluded that they were in a hurry for us to eat and leave. If so, it didn't work. We enjoyed a leisurely meal, Gene had his usual smoke and just before closing time we strolled nonchalantly back to our motel room.

On the following morning, the lady who was in charge of the program that we were to deliver arrived at the motel to take us to the work site. She stopped at the front desk and asked for me. The desk clerk told her that he would get me on the phone, which he did. I answered by saying, "We are in room 106. Come on around and pick us up."

We immediately heard the voice of the desk clerk who had been listening to our conversation from his extension who interjected, "She will have to pick you up in the front. She can't come to your room."

I thought to myself, "This is one sick man." As it happened, this was not the last time that I would experience the same kind of prejudicial thinking. Generally, I found it amusing, but now and then it was quite an inconvenience.

When Gene and I presented at major conferences or conventions, we would be allotted a block of time, usually a one to one and a half hour block during which we would provide a single co-ordinated program. Gene would always present first, because he was very skilled at getting an audience to open itself to hear whatever might come next. He could find humor in the simplest of things, and his down-to-earth manner moved people away from their own piety and self-consciousness toward being more at ease with themselves and with those around them. I would always follow Gene and would take on some issues that were difficult for most people to discuss. I always sprinkled my message generously with humor, but I never told a humorous story unless it carried some message that I wanted to get over. My brother-in-law, Hornsby Howell used to say to me,"You are joking facts." I became aware that I was indeed "joking facts", and that the cold hard facts of life were easier to take when they were delivered with humor and a total absence of blaming and finger pointing.

In my bank of things worth remembering are hundreds of Gene and Dudley episodes, many of which are best left to rest, because of the embarrassment that they may cause to someone who through our influence later became a more open-minded citizen and a productive school administrator. There are still others that I will not discuss, because someone else needed the credit for work that we did, and we willingly allowed them to have that credit. There were still other instances in which our best efforts produced no noticeable change in someone's attitudes. In either case, we were so busy moving on to the next assignment that we took no time to enjoy the praise or to dignify the criticism of those who made judgments of our work.

At the time of this writing, Gene and I remain the best of friends. It has been several weeks since I have seen Gene even though we live only 15 miles apart. If I should run into him today, we would begin exactly where we left off the last time that we were together. For me, this is the truest measure of friendship.

The Challenge of Second Generation Desegregation

The move from a dual to a unitary school system was much easier to accomplish than was the next phase of providing equal access to education for all children. This phase had been comparable to making a place at the table for all members of the family. Having done so does not assure that all will have a good meal. Some will be more skilled than others at negotiating for the food, and some may receive preferential treatment from the food server. So it was with the educational enterprise. The law could not protect a child against prejudice, nor could it police every classroom to see if some children were being denied equal access to knowledge. The only strategy that we could employ was that of providing training aimed at making educators more sensitive to the new environment in which they were working; and exposing them to the practices and techniques that seemed to work best with heterogeneous groups of children. This new direction led the Division of Human Relations toward a new focus.

Upon becoming the Assistant State Superintendent for Human Relations and Student Affairs, I undertook the task of finding a person to occupy my vacated position as Director of the Division of Human Relations. In our first round of interviews for that position, the person that stood out was Major Boyd from Kinston. Major had similar duties in the Kinston City Schools, and his temperament seemed suited for the work that was ahead for the Division. However, Major was offered an opportunity to go to school and complete his terminal degree, so he did not accept the job offer. The recruitment process was re-opened. This time we were led to Lee Grier who was then working at Saint Augustine's College in its' Technical Assistance Center. Lee accepted the challenge to change the thrust of the Division from crisis prevention and intervention to that of providing training in the area of Human Relations.

Under the leadership of Lee Grier and Odell Watson, the assistant director, the Division became quite successful at helping school systems with programs for all school personnel. The major focus was on teaching, but much of our work was done with administrators and with non-certified personnel. We sometimes worked directly with students in helping them to organize and implement programs in student affairs in their respective schools, but this was successful only to the degree that local leadership was available to continue these programs after our people had left the school. The Division expanded its personnel to include female and American Indian members of the team. Two of the early members of the Division who had worked closely with me, Thomasine Hardy and Reeves McGlohon, were still in the Department, though each had taken on other duties. They offered the benefit of their experiences as the new direction was established.

The work of the Division of Human Relations would continue through the eighties. By the early nineties, the Federal Government began to lessen its support for our program, because it determined that no crisis existed in North Carolina and that its money was needed more elsewhere in the nation. The State funding, which consisted mostly of in-kind support, had never been sufficient to sustain the Division.

So, in the early nineties, the Division was dismantled. Prior to that having taken place, it had experienced a period of total redirection. Lee Grier had moved to another division. Odell Watson had taken on another role. Oliver Johnson and Donald Farthing, who had been the longest tenured members of the Division, had left for other positions. By the year 1985, the Division existed only through the work that I personally did from my office.

In 1986, we applied again for some Federal money that had become available, and we were successful in being able to re-establish a technical assistance team within the Department. By that time, I had been named Associate State Superintendent for Public Affairs, but State Superintendent Craig Phillips asked me to take the lead responsibility for that effort since I was experienced in, and committed to, that area of activity. I was able to attract a great educational leader, William Newkirk, to lead that newly established team. He added Jay Cannon as his assistant, and the team began immediately to restore the high priority of providing technical assistance that had been a staple of the Craig Phillips years. The efforts we made to desegregate schools, establish equal status relationships and ensure that every child had an equal opportunity for a quality education bore good fruit, but it lasted only until the retirement of Craig Phillips. When Craig left at the end of 1988, there was no champion of these concepts. So, the idea whose time had passed it by, died without notice.

When I reflect on the twenty-one years that I spent in the Department of Public Instruction, the only real contribution that I am certain that I made was that of bringing people together and helping them to be more respectful of each other. I still spend my energy in that direction, but I now have the feeling that the will to improve relations is at a very low point in our recent history. I can see no concerted effort on the part of any designated group or office to do so. The need is certainly as great as it has ever been, but since it is a silent crisis, the solution may have to wait for overt strife to generate its re-emergence.

My Years at NCASA

In the year 1987, Craig Phillips made it known that he would not seek re-election at the end of his term that would end on December 31,1988. When the announcement was made, a good number of people called me offering their support should I elect to run for the position of State Superintendent. I was honored that so many educators saw me as someone that should hold that position. However, having worked so closely with Craig Phillips, I knew enough about the job to realize that I was not well-suited for it. The least attractive aspect of that job to me was the campaigning for office. The next least attractive part was the lobbying of the General Assembly for the money needed to support public education. Absent these two responsibilities, the office would have been very attractive to me.

Speculation had spread around the government complex that I might seek the office of State

Superintendent of Public Instruction. I did nothing to generate the speculation, but since Craig had no heir apparent, as do most outgoing long-tenured office holders, I emerged in the minds of some people as that person. Speculation reached such a level that I was sent a message by some leaders in the Democratic Party that there was growing support for me to run for the position of Secretary of State, but that Bob Etheridge was considering a run for State Superintendent and they hoped that there would be no opposition to his candidacy. I thought it strange that I, an educator, would have been seen as acceptable for the office of Secretary of State, but not for the lead position in my own field. However, since I had no plans to seek any elected office, I thanked the persons who had contacted me and assured them that I would not become a candidate for either office.

Shortly after the official campaign season opened, Mr. Etheridge came to my office to meet with me. He shared with me the fact that he was considering running for State Superintendent and that he would like my opinion and advice on that issue. I pointed out to him that he had been an excellent legislator, unusually well-respected by educators because of his consistent support for education while serving in the General Assembly. I told him that I recognized that the next State Superintendent would have to have a good rapport with the General Assembly, and that if he were to take on that role and make that the centerpiece of his administration, he would most likely be successful. I told him that he would do well to find the most highly respected educational administrator in the state and make him or her the highest-ranking member of his management team, thus freeing himself from the day-to-day operations of the educational complex.

Bob Etheridge was elected State Superintendent in the 1988 election, and proceeded to put together his own leadership team. I was asked to serve as his Ombudsman, a position that capitalized on my previous contacts around the state and nation, and on my communication skills. I was initially involved in the decision-making process, but as the new administration took shape, my role became less critical. I found my strengths and experiences becoming inconsistent with the prevailing direction that the agency seemed to be heading, so I made the decision to retire from the agency. I had not announced my decision to anyone except my administrative assistant, Shelia White, and my wife. At that point, I was convinced that these two were the only two people left who would care one way or the other about my decision to leave. Then, fate intervened.

In the month of November, the Department held its quarterly meeting of local superintendents in Raleigh. I had no part in the program, a fact to which I had become accustomed. I went to the meeting only because I knew that it would be the last such meeting for me. After twenty-one years in the agency, I had developed some very special relationships with the educational leaders of the state, and I wanted to see them one last time before going out on my own. My plans were to open my own speaking and consulting practice. I already had some major successes in that arena, and I had always known that I would follow that path upon my retirement.

While the meeting was in recess, I was visiting with some friends in the hall when Dr. James Causby, then Superintendent of Polk County Schools approached me. Jim asked me if I would be interested in applying for the position of Executive Director of the North Carolina Association of School Administrators. I shared with Jim that I had not been aware that the position was open, but would give it some thought. Later that same day, Dr. John Dunn, Superintendent of Edenton-Chowan County Schools, asked me to apply for the same position. These were two men for whom I had great respect. Later that evening, I received calls at home from Jerry Pascal, Superintendent of Whiteville City Schools, and from Trudy Blake, who was the sitting NCASA President. After those calls, I agreed to look seriously at that position.

On the following Monday, I called Ossie Fields who worked for NCASA and made an appointment to talk with him about where the organization was and where it seemed to be heading. Ossie was truthful with me about all the problems that would confront the next chief executive officer of the organization, and hearing those challenges helped me to know that I would have the opportunity to be on the cutting edge of the effort to improve education in our state. I applied for the position, was hired, and began work for the Association on January 1, 1991, only one day after my departure from SDPI. I was happy to be going to something as opposed to going away from something as my reason for leaving the Department.

The first few weeks on my new job were hectic. I had a lot to learn about the status of our finances, the expectations of our membership, the opportunities for interaction with our peer organizations and the development of relationships with groups that we needed as allies. My staff consisted of one full-time office manager, Joyce Myers, who had been with the Association for about four years prior to my coming, and one part-time worker, Ossie Fields. Ossie was scheduled to work one day a week, but he frequently came in when there was a time-sensitive task to be done. He managed our financial affairs, our newsletter, and our insurance programs. He also worked with our Retired Superintendents Division on all of its activities.

When I began work for NCASA in 1991, its active membership was 623. Its annual budget had been set at $153,280. However, its income for that year was $127,971. So, my first challenge was to balance the budget. This we did within one year. My next act was to hold a planning session with the Board of Directors during which we established specific objectives for the organization to be reached over a five-year period. We also developed strategies for reaching those objectives.

By the 1994-95 membership year, NCASA membership surpassed 3,000. It had expanded from its two divisions of Superintendents and General Administrators to include divisions for Principals/Assistant Principals, Personnel Officers, Professors of Higher Education, Vocational Directors and Finance Officers. The following year, we added the division for Directors of Exceptional Children. Finally, there was an organization available for any school administrator in our state to call home. There still existed other organizations designed to serve particular groups of administrators, but NCASA had established itself as the organization that spoke most clearly and most forcefully on those matters of concern to school administrators. When these things were achieved, I felt that it was time for me to step down from the leadership role so that new leadership could take the organization into the next critical phase of its work. On March 31, 1996, I retired from the Executive Director position of NCASA. I knew that I was leaving the organization in good condition and in good hands.

The Years Since NCASA

During the years that I worked with athletics, I had a favorite expression that I used to motivate the players. It was, "This is winning time". I used this expression to refer to the last quarter of the game. Whether it was football or basketball, we knew that we could not win a game in the first three quarters. We had to use that time to put ourselves in position to win in the last quarter of the game. We further noted that if we lost the game, no one would remember how well we had played the first three quarters. If we won the game, few would long remember how poorly we might have performed in the earlier stages.

So it has been with me in the game of life. It is said that we are promised three score and ten years, unless by an unusual blessing we receive an extension to four score years. Now that I have achieved that extension and have celebrated my 80th birthday, that clearly places me in the fourth quarter of my life. So, for me, this is winning time. This is the time when one must take stock of all that one has experienced, narrow one's focus on a few targets and go "full-court press" at achieving them. For me, those targets are clear. I want nothing more than to be an example for young, aspiring educators that you can have a successful and enjoyable life while working in that field of service. You can make a difference in the lives of others if you commit to doing so. You will be appreciated much more than those that you have helped along the way will ever tell you. You can find inner peace in knowing that you have done your best to leave the world a better place than it was when you found it.

I have been blessed with a gift for oratory. I have been further blessed with the opportunity to practice this art throughout the nation and in three foreign countries. I have spoken to audiences in each of North Carolina's 100 counties, and in each of the fifty United States with the exception of the states of South Dakota and Montana. I have had people in my workshops that lived in those two states. So, I have had some influence on education in them, even though I have not been there physically. From this point on, I plan to concentrate on speaking and writing about the things that are most important to me. I do not expect to publish anything that will become a great commercial success. I simply want to share my experiences with anyone who is trying to improve the world in which we live. In this way, I hope to repay some of the debt that I owe to my family that has supported me, to my friends that have inspired me and to my late wife, who for fifty-five years and four months, was my partner, helper, strength and confidant…and most of all, to the angel by whom I was raised, my beloved mother.

CPSIA information can be obtained
at www.ICGtesting.com
Printed in the USA
LVHW102037211022
731248LV00001B/34